Hymn and Scripture Selection Guide

Compiled by DONALD A. SPENCER

A Cross-Reference of Scripture and Hymns
with over 12,000 References
for 380 Hymns and Gospel Songs

Judson Press ® Valley Forge

HOUSTON PUBLIC LIBRARY

To my wife
BARBARA
and our children
TODD, AMY, and STEPHANIE

HYMN AND SCRIPTURE SELECTION GUIDE

Copyright © 1977
Judson Press, Valley Forge, PA 19481

Library of Congress Cataloging in Publication Data

Spencer, Donald Amos, 1945-
    Hymn and Scripture selection guide.

    Includes index.
    1. Hymns, English—History and criticism.
2.   Bible—Use in hymns.   I. Title.
BV312.S67   264'.2   76-48529
ISBN 0-8170-0705-9

The name JUDSON PRESS is registered as a trademark in the U.S. Patent Office.

Printed in the U.S.A.

Preface

The awesome responsibility of selecting hymns carefully for a service of worship or other church programs is a task that is often taken too lightly. Leaders should exert extreme care in executing this task if singing is to have its fullest meaning. Some leaders choose hymns with little or no regard for their suitability to the Scripture or the emphasis of a program or service. A leader should always take pains to search out the appropriate hymns, although at times information about a sermon, program topic, or text comes at the last minute so that there is not adequate time to select hymns carefully. The job may seem to be overwhelming, and one may feel that the results are not worth the effort and time that could well be used for other tasks. Even so, the correlation of hymns and Scripture is important for meaningful worship.

What is the answer, then? The ideal way is thorough knowledge of both the Scriptures and the content of a large number of hymns. The traditional practice has been to begin with a familiarity with the Scriptures and a comparison with whatever topical headings and indexes are included in the hymnbook. This method offers a partial solution if used to full advantage, but it does not always lead to a realization of the scriptural foundations for many of our hymns. This relationship must be taken into consideration, since the basic teachings and practices of the Christian faith are dependent upon Scripture. Moreover, relating Scripture to specific hymns will enhance the singers' understanding and appreciation and will add meaning to any service or program. Also, each particular hymn or

Scripture passage used will glow with added meaning.

To meet this need, this book has been designed for pastors, ministers of music, choir directors, and leaders of any church-related organization.

The decision of how many hymns and which ones should be included in this book has been made by examining the hymnals representing ten major denominations as well as five widely used interdenominational hymnals. To have included all hymns from all of these hymnals would have resulted in a book that would have been too large to be of any practical use. Therefore, the hymns included are generally limited to those that appear in at least five of the hymnals examined. It is likely that more than half of the hymns in this book will be found in almost any hymnal, making this book an invaluable tool.

In the first section of this book, the hymns are presented in alphabetical order. The related Scripture passages, taken from the Old and New Testaments as commonly in use by American Protestant denominations, are listed under each hymn. For practical purposes, the number of references is limited. Passages that are directly related to a hymn, such as paraphrases and direct quotations, are shown in italics. Under the title of each hymn there are topical headings and summary phrases that are intended to show the relationship between the hymn and the Scripture passage.

In the second section of this book is a listing of Scripture passages in their order as found in the Bible. Under each of these are hymns or stanzas that are, or could be, appropriate to that passage. The numbers given with each such passage are the numbers of the hymns in the first section. Although numerous hymns could have been listed for any given text, those that are less appropriate have been omitted. Many more Scripture references are included in this section than in the first section. Thus, the person beginning with a Scripture passage can find a suitable hymn. However, beginning with the hymn by using the first section gives a finer selection of passages that are appropriate. For quick location of a hymn, an index of hymn titles is provided in the final pages of the book.

Because some references apply to particular stanzas or phrases and some Scripture passages may have varied uses, all hymns and Scripture references should be chosen with the particular emphasis desired in mind.

Hymnals vary; therefore, if a stanza reference is given and the relationship is not apparent, the other stanzas of the hymn should be examined since occasional additions or deletions of stanzas occur in some hymnals. Generally, references to stanzas are given only when the arrangement of stanzas is the same in the majority of the hymnals examined.

In almost every case, many Scripture passages of marginal correspondence that could be listed for a hymn have been omitted. The effort of this work is merely to provide an adequate number of references for each hymn so that the book will not be too unwieldly to be useful. The user of the book may want to write in the margins additional Scripture references, notes, references to poems, comments, or similar information that one has found useful with a particular hymn.

Throughout the almost eight years spent in compiling this work, it has been my prayer that God would lead and guide my thoughts and research. It is now my prayer that as this book is used, it will be an effective tool in making congregational singing more meaningful. "I will sing with the spirit, and I will sing with the understanding also" (1 Corinthians 14:15, KJV).

Donald A. Spencer

Section A

Hymns with
Scripture References

1—A CHARGE TO KEEP I HAVE
Expression of commitment to a victorious life and to serve God faithfully

Josh. 24:15; John 12:26; Eph. 2:10; 4:1; 1 Pet. 4:10-11
St. 1—John 15:8; 1 Cor. 6:20
St. 2—Eph. 5:17
St. 3—Rom. 14:12; 2 Cor. 5:9-10
St. 4—Eph. 6:10; Phil. 3:14

2—A CHILD OF THE KING
Adoption as sons as our relationship with God

Rom. 8:14-17; Gal. 4:1-7; Eph. 1:5; James 2:5

3—A MIGHTY FORTRESS IS OUR GOD
Majesty and power of God; lordship of Christ; God as our refuge and strength; Christian warfare

Ps. 46
Deut. 33:27; 2 Sam. 22:2; Isa. 26:4; 40:28
St. 1—Ps. 46:1
St. 2—Hab. 3:18-19; Rom. 1:17; 5:12-21
St. 3—Luke 11:20-22; Col. 2:15; Heb. 2:14-18
St. 4—Dan. 4:3; Matt. 12:20-21; Gal. 5:22-23; Phil. 2:9

A RULER ONCE CAME TO JESUS—See **YE MUST BE BORN AGAIN**

A WONDERFUL SAVIOR IS JESUS—See **HE HIDETH MY SOUL**

4—ABIDE WITH ME
Evening; peace and comfort; God's presence in life and death

Ps. 23:4; 92:2; 139:7-12; 145:18; Matt. 28:20; Luke 24:29; 1 John 3:24

5—ACCORDING TO THY GRACIOUS WORD
Remembrance of the Lord's Supper

Luke 22:19-20
Matt. 26:26-29; John 6:53-58; 1 Cor. 11:23-28
St. 4—Luke 23:42

6—AH, HOLY JESUS, HOW HAST THOU OFFENDED
Praise for Jesus' suffering and death for our sins; incarnation

Isa. 53; John 10:11; 19:17-30; Rom. 5:6-11; Gal. 3:13; 1 Pet. 3:18; 4:13

7—ALAS, AND DID MY SAVIOR BLEED
Atonement; cross of Christ; salvation

Isa. 53; John 19:17-18; Rom. 5:6-11; 2 Cor. 5:14; Eph. 1:7; 2:13; Col. 1:11-23; Titus 2:14; Heb. 1:3; 9:12-26; 1 John 1:7; 4:19

8—ALL CREATURES OF OUR GOD AND KING
Worship; praise and adoration to God as Creator

Ps. 96:1-6; 148
Ps. 97:6; 117; 136:1-9; 145:10-13; 150:6; Jer. 32:17-20; Rom. 11:36; 1 Cor. 8:6; Rev. 4:11; 14:7

9—ALL FOR JESUS
Expression of total and complete consecration

Matt. 22:37; Mark 10:28; Rom. 6:13, 19; 12:1-2; 2 Cor. 5:15
St. 3—1 Cor. 2:2; Phil. 3:7-8
St. 4—1 Thess. 1:4; Rev. 17:14

10—ALL GLORY, LAUD, AND HONOR
Palm Sunday; praise to Christ as King

Matt. 21:1-9; Mark 11:1-10; Luke 19:29-38; John 12:12-13; Rev. 5:12; 7:9-12

11—ALL HAIL THE POWER OF JESUS' NAME
Praise to Christ as Lord and King; name of Christ

Isa. 9:6; Col. 1:15-19; Phil. 2:9-11; Heb. 2:7-8; Rev. 5:13; 11:15
St. 1 & 4—Ps. 148:2; Heb. 1:6; Rev. 5:11-12; 7:11-12
St. 2—Deut. 7:6; Isa. 41:8-9; Rom. 8:29-30; Eph. 1:4-6; Rev. 17:14
St. 3—Ps. 66:1; 145:21; Isa. 61:11; Heb. 2:12

12—ALL MY HEART THIS NIGHT REJOICES
Christmas; angels proclaim the birth of Jesus

Luke 1:14; 2:8-20; 2:11

13—ALL PEOPLE THAT ON EARTH DO DWELL
Joyful praise and adoration for the loving care and guidance of an omnipotent God

Ps. 100—paraphrase
Ps. 2:11; 97:1; 98:3-4; 150:6; Jer. 33:11
St. 1—Ps. 100:1-2
St. 2—Ps. 100:3
St. 3—Ps. 100:4
St. 4—Ps. 100:5

14—ALL PRAISE TO THEE, MY GOD, THIS NIGHT
Evening: thanks for day; prayer of forgiveness and for freedom from fear of death

Ps. 4:8; 42:8; 63:6; 92:1-2; Prov. 3:24; Luke 24:29; 1 Thess. 4:14

ALL PRAISE TO HIM WHO REIGNS—See BLESSED BE THE NAME

15—ALL THE WAY MY SAVIOR LEADS
Assurance and trust in Jesus' guidance and leadership in life

Ps. 32:8; John 10:3-5; 12:26; 14:18, 27; 2 Cor. 3:5; 12:9; Rev. 7:17
St. 2—John 4:14; 6:32-35; 1 Cor. 10:4
St. 3—Isa. 35:10; John 14:1-3; Heb. 4:9

16—ALL THINGS ARE THINE
Stewardship; church dedication

1 Chron. 29:14; Hag. 2:8-9
Gen. 28:22; Lev. 27:30-33; 1 Kings 8:13; 2 Chron. 2:4; *(next page)*

Mal. 3:8-10; 1 Cor. 16:2

17—ALL THINGS BRIGHT AND BEAUTIFUL
Praise and adoration for the beauty and blessings of God's creation
Neh. 9:6; Ps. 19:1-8; 104:24; 136:3-9; Rom. 1:20; Heb. 11:3; Rev. 4:11

ALL TO JESUS I SURRENDER—See I SURRENDER ALL

ALMIGHTY FATHER, STRONG TO SAVE—See ETERNAL FATHER . . .

18—AM I A SOLDIER OF THE CROSS
Expression of commitment to endure and do our part as good soldiers of Jesus Christ

1 Cor. 16:13; Eph. 6:10-20; Phil. 1:27-30; 1 Tim. 6:12; 2 Tim. 2:3-4; Heb. 10:23; Jude 3

19—AMAZING GRACE
God's infinite grace

John 1:16-17; Rom. 5:20-21; 1 Cor. 15:10; 2 Cor. 12:9; Eph. 1:6-7; Titus 2:11
St. 4—Ps. 145:1-2

20—ANGELS FROM THE REALMS OF GLORY
Birth of Christ; shepherds, wise men, angels—all came to worship the newborn King.

Matt. 2:11; Luke 2:15; Heb. 1:6
St. 1—Job 38:7; Luke 2:10-14
St. 2—Isa. 7:14; Matt. 1:23; Luke 2:8-20; John 1:9
St. 3—Hag. 2:7; Matt 2:1-12
St. 4—Hag. 2:7; Mal. 3:1; 1 Thess. 4:16

21—ANGELS WE HAVE HEARD ON HIGH
Birth of Christ; shepherds and angels

Luke 2:7-20
Refrain—Luke 2:14

22—"ARE YE ABLE," SAID THE MASTER
Expression of complete consecration

Matt. 20:22; Mark 8:34; Luke 14:27; John 12:26
St. 2—Luke 23:39-43
St. 3—Eccl. 12:7

23—ARE YOU WASHED IN THE BLOOD
By God's grace we are cleansed by the blood of the Lamb.

Ps. 51:2, 7; Isa. 1:18; Eph. 1:6-8; Col. 1:14; Titus 3:5-7; Heb. 9:14;
1 John 1:7-9

24—ARISE, MY SOUL, ARISE
Atonement; reconciliation through Christ; sonship to God

Isa. 53:5; Eph. 2:13; 1 Tim. 2:5; Titus 3:5-7; Heb. 2:14-15; 7:25; 9:15, 24
St. 1—Isa. 12:2; 43:1; Heb. 10:12
St. 2—Rom. 3:25-26; Heb. 4:16
St. 3—John 20:20, 25
St. 4 & 5—John 1:12-13; Rom. 8:14-17; 2 Cor. 5:19; Gal. 4:6

ART THOU WEARY, ART THOU LANGUID—See ART THOU WEARY, HEAVY LADEN

25—ART THOU WEARY, HEAVY LADEN
Rest and guidance sought from Jesus

Matt. 11:28
Exod. 33:14; Ps. 23:2; 55:22; Isa. 14:3; Heb. 4:1-11
St. 2—John 20:25-27

26—AS PANTS THE HART
Closeness to God; desire of our soul for refreshing

Ps. 42:1-2, 5, 9, 11
Ps. 63:1; 85:6; 143:6; John 4:14; Acts 17:27
St. 4—Ps. 71:14

27—AS WITH GLADNESS MEN OF OLD
Christmas; prayer that we may be led to Christ just as the wise men

Matt. 2:1-12; Eph. 1:3-4

28—ASK YE WHAT GREAT THING I KNOW
Faith; joy; praise of Christ, the crucified; name of Christ

1 Cor. 2:2

Mark 5:19; John 3:16-17; Acts 2:36; Rom. 5:1; 1 Cor. 1:31; 1 Cor. 3:11; Gal. 2:20; 1 Pet. 3:15

29—AT CALVARY
Atonement; salvation; God's love and grace as expressed through Christ's suffering and death on the cross

Luke 23:33; Rom. 5:6-11; 1 Cor. 1:18; Eph. 2:13-18; 5:2; Col. 1:20-23; 1 Tim. 1:13; 1 Pet. 1:25; 1 John 4:10; Rev. 1:5-6

30—AT THE CROSS
Atonement; salvation; cross of Jesus

Isa. 53; John 19:17-18; Rom. 5:6-11; 2 Cor. 5:14; Eph. 1:7; Eph. 2:13; Col. 1:11-23; Titus 2:14; Heb. 1:3; 9:12-26; 1 John 1:7; 4:19

31—AT THE NAME OF JESUS
Name of Jesus; humanity and lordship of Christ; expression of submission to Christ

Phil. 2:5-11

Isa. 45:23; Matt. 1:21; Acts 4:12; Heb. 1:4
St. 1—Isa. 45:23; John 1:1; Phil. 2:10-11
St. 2—Gen. 1:1; John 1:1-3
St. 3—Rom. 8:3; Phil. 2:7-8
St. 4—Heb. 2:10; James 1:12

32—AWAKE, MY SOUL, AND WITH THE SUN
Morning; facing a new day renewed

Ps. 5:3; 61:8; 92:2; 108:2-3; Mal. 1:11; John 9:4; Rom. 13:12; 1 Thess. 5:4-6

33—AWAKE, MY SOUL, IN JOYFUL LAYS
Worship; praise and adoration for God's love, mercy, and kindness as shown in redemption and in his providential care

Exod. 34:6; Ps. 63:3; 107:43; 136; 138:2
St. 1—Ps. 92:2-4; 101:1; 136:1-4; Isa. 63:7-9
St. 2—John 3:16-17; Rom. 5:6-11; Eph. 2:7; Titus 3:3-7

St. 3—Ps. 26:11-12; 36:7; 40:11; 136:23-24; 139:9-10; Rom. 8:38-39
St. 4—Ps. 31:21; 86:15; 89:30-33; Rom. 8:38-39

34—AWAKE, MY SOUL, STRETCH EVERY NERVE
God calls us to run the race and receive our reward.

Heb. 12:1-2
1 Cor. 9:24; Phil. 2:16; 3:12-14

35—AWAY IN A MANGER
Birth of Christ; children

Luke 2:7, 12, 16; Mark 10:13-16

BE NOT DISMAYED—See GOD WILL TAKE CARE OF YOU

36—BE STILL, MY SOUL
In the midst of life our strength comes from a quiet confidence in God's leadership.

Ps. 46:10
Ps. 27; 37:3-5; 118:8; Prov. 3:5; Isa. 30:15; Heb. 10:35
St. 1—John 15:14-15
St. 2—Ps. 107:29; Mark 4:37-41; Heb. 7:24
St. 3—Rev. 7:17; 21:4

37—BE THOU MY VISION
God's care, guidance, and example; unity with God

Ps. 17:15; 148:13; Prov. 29:18; Hos. 12:6; Matt. 5:48; 13:44; 19:21; John 14:20; 17:21; Rom. 8:14; 1 Cor. 8:6; Eph. 2:13-22; 4:4-6; Phil. 3:12; Heb. 7:26; 1 Pet. 2:21; 1 John 3; 4:13

38—BEFORE JEHOVAH'S AWFUL THRONE
Worship; praise to God as Creator and Supreme

Ps. 100—paraphrase
Ps. 83:18; 96; 103:19
St. 1—Ps. 100:1-3; Deut. 4:39
St. 2—Ps. 100:3; 1 Pet. 2:25; Matt. 18:11-14
St. 3—Ps. 100:4
St. 4—Deut. 32:4; Ps. 100:5

39—BEGIN, MY TONGUE, SOME HEAVENLY THEME
Faithfulness and boundlessness of God's mercy and love

1 Chron. 16:8; Ps. 9:11; 19:1; 26:7; 35:28; 40:10-11; 85:5, 8; 89:1; 106:1-2; 145; Isa. 12:4-5; Matt. 7:11; John 15:27; 1 Pet. 1:3-6

40—BENEATH THE CROSS OF JESUS
We take our stand beneath the cross of Christ and express those things we feel when thinking of the cross.

Isa. 32:2; Luke 9:23; 1 Cor. 1:17-18; Gal. 6:14

41—BLESSED ASSURANCE
Joy of the new life in Christ; submission to God

Isa. 12:2; Rom. 8:16-17; 15:13; 2 Cor. 5:17; 1 Thess. 2:19-20; Titus 2:13; 3:5-7; Heb. 6:19; 1 Pet. 1:7-9; 2:3; Rev. 1:5-6
Refrain—Ps. 40:3; James 5:13

42—BLESSED BE THE NAME
Reign of Christ; praise to Christ as Savior; name of Christ; blood of Christ

Ps. 7:17; 71:23; Matt. 12:21; Acts 4:12; Phil. 2:9-11; Heb. 1:3-4; Rev. 5:12
St. 3—Isa. 1:18; Rom. 8:1-2; Col. 1:14; Rev. 1:5

43—BLESSED JESUS, AT THY WORD
Through Jesus and with aid of the Holy Spirit, we approach God in worship.

Luke 11:28
St. 2—1 Cor. 2:10; Eph. 2:18
St. 3—2 Sam. 22:29; Ps. 34:15

44—BLEST BE THE TIE THAT BINDS
Mutual concern and fellowship of Christians

Ps. 133:1; Matt. 18:20; John 13:34-35; Rom. 12:5; 15:1-2; Gal. 3:28; 6:2; Col. 2:2; Heb. 13:1; 1 Pet. 3:8

45—BOOK OF BOOKS, OUR PEOPLE'S STRENGTH
Importance of Bible, the word of God

Ps. 19:7-8; Luke 24:27; 1 Thess. 2:13; 2 Tim. 3:16-17; 2 Pet. 1:19-21;

Rev. 1:3
St. 1—Ps. 119:105, 130; 2 Tim. 3:16-17
St. 2—Ps. 102:18; Heb. 1:1
St. 3—Ps. 102:18; John 1:14

46—BREAD OF THE WORLD IN MERCY BROKEN
Lord's Supper; meaning of bread and wine; prayer expressing desire
to remember God's grace

John 6:51
Matt. 26:26-29; Luke 24:30; John 6:58; 1 Cor. 11:23-28

47—BREAK THOU THE BREAD OF LIFE
Jesus' feeding of multitude compared to his feeding us through his
Word; prayer that God's Spirit will help us to understand the Bible

Deut. 8:3; Jer. 15:16; Matt. 4:4; 14:13-21; John 6:35
St. 1—John 5:39
St. 2—Ps. 119:45; John 8:32
St. 3—Luke 24:32; John 17:17; 2 Tim. 3:15-16
St. 4—Luke 24:45; 1 Cor. 2:10-13; 2 Pet. 1:20-21

48—BREATHE ON ME
Holy Spirit; prayer; aspiration; unity of our will with God's will

John 20:22
Job 33:4; Ezek. 36:27; John 3:5-7; Rom. 8:9-11; 2 Cor. 3:18; Gal. 5:5,
17-18, 22-25; Eph. 4:3; 1 John 4:13

49—BRIGHTEST AND BEST
Birth of Christ; the star leads to the true Light; we praise him and
offer our gifts.

Matt. 2:1-12
St. 1—Matt. 2:9-10; Luke 1:77-79
St. 2—Luke 2:7, 11-12
St. 3—Matt. 2:11
St. 4—Luke 1:46-47

50—BUILT ON THE ROCK
Christ as foundation of church and present in its worship; our bodies
as the temple of Christ

Matt. 16:18; 1 Cor. 3:11; 10:4; Eph. 1:22-23; 2:19-22; Col. 1:18

St. 2 & 3—Matt. 18:20; Acts 7:48; 17:24; 1 Cor. 3:16; 6:19

51—CHILDREN OF THE HEAVENLY FATHER
God's guidance and care of his children

Matt. 18:14; Gal. 3:26; 2 Thess. 3:3; 2 Tim. 4:18; 1 Pet. 5:10
St. 1—Prov. 14:26
St. 2—Gen. 50:21; Acts 2:25; 2 Thess. 3:3
St. 3—John 10:28; Rom. 8:35-39
St. 4—Job 1:21; Ps. 37:28; Prov. 2:8; 1 Thess. 5:23

52—CHILDREN OF THE HEAVENLY KING
As children of the heavenly King we follow Christ as leader and give him praise; our hope for the future

Ps. 48:14; 104:33; Isa. 35:10; Gal. 3:26; Col. 3:15-17; 1 John 3:2

53—CHRIST AROSE
Resurrection of Christ; joy; praise to Christ for his victory over death and the grave

Acts 13:29-30; 1 Cor. 15:4
St. 1 & 2—Matt. 27:57-66; Mark 15:46-47; John 19:41-42
St. 3 & refrain—Matt. 28:1-9; Mark 16:1-6; Luke 24:1-7;
                Acts 2:24, 32; Rom. 6:9; 14:9

54—CHRIST FOR THE WORLD WE SING
Worldwide missions

Ps. 22:27; 40:3; Mark 13:10; 16:15; Acts 1:8; Rom. 10:12-15;
1 Pet. 4:10-11; 1 John 5:4-5
St. 4—Isa. 51:11; Rev. 14:3

55—CHRIST IS MADE THE SURE FOUNDATION
The church's foundation is Jesus Christ; invocation; praise; church dedication

Mark 12:10; 1 Cor. 3:11; Eph. 1:22-23; 2:20-22; Col. 1:18; 2 Tim. 2:19
St. 2—Ps. 18:6; 1 Pet. 3:12
St. 3—2 Tim. 1:12; 2:12; 1 Pet. 1:5; Rev. 22:5

56—CHRIST IS THE WORLD'S TRUE LIGHT
World unity in Christ; universal gospel; missions

John 1:4-5, 9; 8:12; 1 Cor. 8:6; 12:13; Col. 3:11
St. 1—John 12:46; Heb. 2:10, 14-15; 2 Pet. 1:19
St. 2—Joel 3:10; Gal. 3:28
St. 3—Prov. 11:2; John 10:16; Acts 5:31; Rev. 11:15

57—CHRIST RECEIVETH SINFUL MEN
By grace we are cleansed and made acceptable to God.

Isa. 55:7; Mic. 7:18-19; Luke 15:2; Acts 10:43; Eph. 1:6-8; 1 Tim. 1:14-15; Titus 2:11; 1 Pet. 4:10
St. 2—Matt. 11:28-29
St. 3—Rom. 6:14; Heb. 9:14

58—CHRIST THE LORD IS RISEN TODAY
Resurrection of Christ; joy; praise; Savior

Acts 2:24-28; 1 Cor. 15:4;
Matt. 28:1-9; Luke 24:1-7
St. 1—Ps. 150:6; Isa. 44:23
St. 2 & 3—Isa. 25:7-8; Rom. 6:9; 1 Cor. 15:54-57
St. 4—Rom. 8:29; 1 Cor. 15:20, 23

CHRIST THOU ART THE SURE FOUNDATION—See CHRIST IS MADE . . .

59—CHRIST WHOSE GLORY FILLS THE SKIES
Worship; morning; Christ as the light of life for the Christian in a world of darkness

Ps. 3; Mal. 4:2; Luke 2:32; John 1:4-9; 8:12; 12:46; Acts 9:3-5; 2 Cor. 4:6; Heb. 1:3; Rev. 21:23

60—COME, CHRISTIANS, JOIN TO SING
Joyful and eternal praise

Ps. 30:4; 67:3; 95:1-2; 145:2; 150:6; Col. 3:16; Heb. 13:15; 1 Pet. 2:9
St. 2—John 15:13
St. 3—Rev. 5:11-13

61—COME, HOLY GHOST, OUR SOULS INSPIRE
The presence, power, and leadership of the Holy Spirit

Ezek. 36:27; Matt. 3:11; Luke 11:13; John 14:16; Acts 2:3-4; 2:38; Rom. 5:5; 8:11-16; 1 Cor. 6:19; Eph. 3:16

62—COME, HOLY SPIRIT, HEAVENLY DOVE
Desire for Holy Spirit to kindle true love in our hearts; our love to God compared to God's love for us

Matt. 3:16; John 6:63; Rom. 5:5; Gal. 5:22
St. 2—Matt. 24:12

63—COME, THOU ALMIGHTY KING
Praise to an omnipotent God, the Word Incarnate and the Holy Spirit that is present in us; acknowledge God's majesty and pledge of our love

Ps. 47:7-8; 51:15; 103:19; 2 Cor. 13:14; 1 Tim. 6:15
St. 1—Exod. 15:18; 1 Chron. 29:11-12; Ps. 83:18; Dan. 7:9, 13, 22
St. 2—Ps. 45:3; John 1:14; Eph. 6:17; Phil. 2:5-7
St. 3—John 14:16-17; Rom. 15:13; Gal. 5:22; 1 Thess. 1:6; Acts 10:38
St. 4—Rom. 14:11

64—COME, THOU FOUNT OF EVERY BLESSING
Aspiration; grace; praise for blessings

Ps. 68:19; 107:8; 116:12; Zech. 13:1; Rom. 5:2; 1 Cor. 15:10; Eph. 1:3; 2 Pet. 1:2; 3:18
St. 2—1 Sam. 7:12; Eph. 1:6-8
St. 3—2 Cor. 1:22; 1 Pet. 2:25

65—COME, THOU LONG-EXPECTED JESUS
Birth of Christ; coming of the long-anticipated Messiah; prayer for redemption through Christ and for his rule in our hearts

Isa. 9:6-7; Dan. 7:13-14; Matt. 1:22-23; 20:28; Luke 1:32-35; 2:1-7

COME, WE THAT LOVE THE LORD—See WE'RE MARCHING TO ZION

66—COME, YE DISCONSOLATE
Invitation to prayer; God can heal, cure, and remove all sorrow and sin's guilt.

John 14:1; 2 Cor. 1:3-7; Heb. 4:16
St. 1—Exod. 25:22
St. 2—John 14:16-18
St. 3—John 6:32-35; Rev. 7:17

67—COME, YE FAITHFUL, RAISE THE STRAIN
Resurrection; exaltation of Christ; praise to risen Savior

Exod. 15:1-21; Isa. 26:19; 42:16; Luke 1:78-79; John 6:40; Acts 2:24-28; Rom. 6:9-10; Eph. 1:14; 2:4-5
St. 2—Isa. 9:2; John 1:5; Col. 1:11-14; Rev. 21:23
St. 3—Ps. 145:13; Rom. 14:11

68—COME, YE THANKFUL PEOPLE, COME
Thanksgiving; harvest hymn; spiritual harvest

1 Chron. 16:8; Ps. 68:19; Ps. 106:1; Matt. 9:37-38; Matt. 13:24-30, 36-43; Heb. 13:15; Rev. 14:15

69—COUNT YOUR BLESSINGS
In all of life's situations we should see these in light of all of the ways God has blessed us.

Ps. 40:5; 68:19; 103:2; 139:17-18; Heb. 6:14; James 1:17
St. 1—Ps. 42:5; Isa. 54:11
St. 2—Ps. 55:22; 1 Pet. 5:7
St. 3—Ps. 49; Prov. 22:2; Matt. 6:19-21; Acts 20:33
St. 4—Ps. 73:23; Isa. 41:13

70—CROWN HIM WITH MANY CROWNS
Christ as Lord and King; our love and praise to Christ; suffering, death, resurrection, and glorification of Christ; peace on earth

Matt. 28:18; Rom. 14:9; Heb. 2:7-10; 12:2; Rev. 1:5-6, 8; 19:1, 12
St. 1—1 Pet. 3:22
St. 2—1 Cor. 15:54-57; 1 John 2:25
St. 3—Isa. 9:6-7
St. 4—John 20:20; 1 John 3:16a; Rev. 1:5

71—DAY BY DAY
We look to God in each day of our lives.

Deut. 33:25; Ps. 55:22; Isa. 14:3; 41:10; John 14:27; 2 Cor. 1:3-5; Phil. 4:13; Heb. 4:16; 1 Pet. 5:7

72—DAY IS DYING IN THE WEST
Evening; adoration; man, nature, and God in communion

Ps. 4:8; 19:1-2; 49:14; 65:8; Isa. 60:19-20; Luke 24:29; John 9:4
Refrain—Ps. 69:34; Isa. 6:3

73—DEAR LORD AND FATHER OF MANKIND
Quiet confidence in God; call of God to service

1 Kings 9:13; Isa. 26:3; 30:15; Mark 1:16-20; 5:15; Eph. 4:6; 2 Tim. 1:9; 1 Pet. 2:9; 1 John 1:9

74—DEPTH OF MERCY! CAN THERE BE
God's great mercy and grace triumphs over our sin

Ps. 86:5; Isa. 55:7; Mic. 7:18-19; Luke 18:13; Rom. 2:4; Eph. 2:4-5; 1 Tim. 1:14-15

DOXOLOGY—See references under ALL PEOPLE THAT ON EARTH DO DWELL

75—DOWN AT THE CROSS
Praise of Christ; blood of Christ; cross of Christ; name of Christ; salvation

Zech. 13:1; Luke 22:20; John 19:17-18; Rom. 5:6-11; Eph. 1:7; 2:13; Col. 1:20-23; Titus 2:14; Heb. 9:12-26; 12:24; 13:15, 20-21; 1 Pet. 2:24; 1 John 1:7; Rev. 1:5-6; 5:9

DRAW ME NEARER—See I AM THINE, O LORD

76—DRAW THOU MY SOUL
Prayer expressing desire of closeness to God and his will

Ps. 40:8; 73:28; 143:10; Matt. 8:19; Acts 17:27; Rom. 12:2; 1 Cor. 6:17; Eph. 1:9-11; Heb. 7:19; 13:21; James 4:8

DYING WITH JESUS—See MOMENT BY MOMENT

ENCAMPED ALONG THE HILLS—See FAITH IS THE VICTORY

77—ETERNAL FATHER, STRONG TO SAVE
God's guidance, care, and protection; Trinity; God of the sea

Ps. 107:23-32
Ps. 57:1; 89:9; 91:2; 95:5; Mark 4:35-41
St. 1—Job 38:10-11
St. 2—Matt. 8:23-27
St. 3—Gen. 1:1-2, 20

St. 4—Ps. 107:31

78—FACE TO FACE
Anticipation of heaven and seeing Christ face to face

1 Cor. 13:12
Isa. 35:10; John 17:24; 2 Cor. 3:18; 5:8; 1 Thess. 4:13-17; 1 John 3:2;
Rev. 21:4; 22:4
St. 3—Isa. 40:3

79—FAIREST LORD JESUS
Praise and adoration of Christ; joy; lordship of Christ

1 Cor. 1:31; Phil. 2:9-11; 1 Tim. 6:16; Heb. 13:8
St. 1—1 Thess. 2:19-20; John 5:23
St. 2—Song of Sol. 2:1; 1 John 3:3
St. 3—John 8:12; Heb. 1:3; Rev. 22:16

80—FAITH IS THE VICTORY
Faith is the victory that overcomes the world; Christian warfare

Gal. 2:20; Eph. 6:10-20; 1 Tim. 6:12; 2 Tim. 2:3-4; 1 John 5:4-5; Jude 3

81—FAITH OF OUR FATHERS
Song of the faith our forefathers had; commitment to win others to
Christ

Jude 3
Ps. 22:4-5; Matt. 24:14; 2 Tim. 4:7; Heb. 11

82—FATHER ETERNAL, RULER OF CREATION
God rules over all his creation; God's will and kingdom will be done.

Matt. 6:10
Ps. 145:13; Acts 14:15; 17:24-26; 1 Pet. 2:17; 1 John 2:17

83—FATHER OF MERCIES, IN THY WORD
We see God's glory and see the Savior in the Word of God; Bible as
our guide

Ps. 19:7-8; 119:18-20, 97; Jer. 15:16; Luke 24:32; John 5:39; Rom.
15:4; 2 Tim. 3:16-17; 2 Pet. 1:9

84—FIGHT THE GOOD FIGHT
Christ is our guide and our strength as we fight the fight of running our course in life.

1 Tim. 6:12
Rom. 8:37; 1 Cor. 9:24-26; 15:57-58; Eph. 6:10-20; Phil. 1:27-30; 3:14; 2 Tim. 2:3-4; 4:7-8; Heb. 10:23; 1 Pet. 5:7-9

85—FLING OUT THE BANNER
The cross as a symbol, banner, or standard and our only hope

Ps. 20:5; 60:4; Isa. 62:10; Gal. 6:14

86—FOR ALL THE SAINTS
Anticipation of joining the saints of the past in heaven

Ps. 22:4-5; Acts 20:32; 1 Thess. 4:13-17; 1 Tim. 6:12; 2 Tim. 4:7; Heb. 4:9; 11:13-16; 1 Pet. 1:3-5; Rev. 6:11; 7:9; 14:13

87—FOR THE BEAUTY OF THE EARTH
Praise and thanksgiving; gratitude for common things in life

Ps. 107:21-22; John 1:3; Phil. 4:8; James 1:17; Rev. 14:7*b*
St. 1 & 2—Gen. 1:11-18; Ps. 19:1-6; 104:24
St. 3—Rom. 12:9-10
St. 4—Col. 3:14; Heb. 13:15

88—FORTH IN THY NAME, O LORD
Prayer for faithfulness to daily service and a consciousness of the inspiring presence of Christ; promise of heaven for those who run the course in true service

Matt. 10:38-39, 42; Luke 17:10; John 12:26; Rom. 12:11; Col. 1:10; 3:17, 24
St. 3—Matt. 11:29-30

89—FROM ALL THAT DWELL BELOW THE SKIES
Worldwide praise of our Creator and Redeemer

Ps. 117—paraphrase
Ps. 67:3; 145:21; 148:5; 150:6; 1 Pet. 2:9; Rev. 15:4

90—FROM EVERY STORMY WIND THAT BLOWS
We look to God and his mercy seat for help in troubles.

Exod. 25:25; Ps. 107:29; Isa. 25:4; 41:10; 2 Cor. 1:3-5; Heb. 4:16
St. 2—Ps. 133:2; Isa. 61:3
St. 3—Ps. 133:1; Eph. 4:13
Last st.—Isa. 40:31

91—FROM GREENLAND'S ICY MOUNTAINS
Worldwide missions

Ps. 22:27; 96:2-3, 10; Matt. 24:14; Mark 13:10; 16:15; Acts 1:8; 16:9-10; Phil. 2:15
St. 3—John 8:12; 12:46

92—FROM HEAVEN ABOVE TO EARTH I COME
Christmas; words of angels to shepherds

Luke 2:10-14

93—FROM THEE ALL SKILL AND SCIENCE FLOW
God is source of human emotion and skills and meets our needs.

Isa. 25:8; Rom. 12:6-8; 1 Cor. 12:4; Eph. 4:11-12; 1 Pet. 4:10-11; Rev. 21:4

94—GENTLE MARY LAID HER CHILD
Birth of Christ; Nativity setting described; praise

Luke 2:7
Matt. 2:1-12; Luke 1:26-28; 2:7-20; Gal. 4:4-5

95—GIVE TO THE WINDS
Expression of trust in God in all of life and its problems

Ps. 37:5; 56:3-4; Isa. 14:3; 41:10; John 14:27; Heb. 4:16; 1 Pet. 5:7

96—GLORIOUS THINGS OF THEE ARE SPOKEN
Zion; church; praise; God's presence in the world and church

Ps. 9:11, 14; 48:1-2; 87:3; Isa. 4:5; 33:20-21
St. 1—Matt. 7:24-25; 16:18
St. 2—John 4:10-14; Rev. 7:17; 22:1, 17
St. 3—Exod. 13:21-22; 33:14; Lev. 26:12

GLORY TO HIS NAME—See DOWN AT THE CROSS

97—GO, LABOR ON, SPEND AND BE SPENT
It is God's will that we evangelize for his glory, not man's.

Luke 14:23; Rom. 12:11; 1 Cor. 15:58; 2 Cor. 12:5; Eph. 2:10
St. 1—1 Pet. 2:21; 1 John 2:6
St. 2—Matt. 5:11-12; John 15:18-19; Gal. 1:10
St. 3—John 9:4
St. 4—Matt. 28:19; Luke 14:23

98—GO TO DARK GETHSEMANE
Christ's prayer, suffering, death, conflict, conquest; lessons in spirit of prayer, bearing the cross, and death

Phil. 3:7-11; Heb. 12:2; 1 Pet. 2:21; 4:12-13
St. 1—Matt. 26:30, 45; Luke 22:44; Col. 4:2
St. 2—John 18:1-40; 19:1-16; 2 Cor. 1:5
St. 3—John 19:17-30; 2 Cor. 5:8
St. 4—John 11:25; 19:31-42; 20:1-18; 1 Cor. 15:22

99—GOD BE WITH YOU
Prayer for God's presence and guidance

Exod. 33:14; Ps. 73:23-24; Acts 20:32; 1 Pet. 5:7
St. 1—Ps. 95:7; Isa. 40:11
St. 2—Deut. 8:3; Ps. 17:8; 57:1; John 6:32-35, 48-51, 58
St. 3—Nah. 1:7; 1 Pet. 4:19
St. 4—Song of Sol. 2:4; Rev. 21:4

100—GOD HIMSELF IS WITH US
Awe in presence of God in worship

Gen. 28:16-17; Ps. 16:8; 33:8; 89:7; Hab. 2:20; John 4:24

101—GOD IS LOVE; HIS MERCY BRIGHTENS
God's love, mercy, and care compared as a light in a world of darkness; comfort; hope; wisdom of God

Neh. 9:17; Ps. 43:3; 103:8, 17; 139:12; Dan. 2:22; Hos. 12:6; Luke 1:78; Acts 26:18; Rom. 8:28; 2 Cor. 4:6; 1 Thess. 5:5; James 1:17; 1 John 1:5, 7; 4:8, 16

102—GOD IS MY STRONG SALVATION
God as our salvation, light, and strength

Ps. 127:1-3

Exod. 15:2; 2 Sam. 22:29; Ps. 29:11; 57:3; Isa. 12:2; 26:3; Mic. 7:8; Eph. 6:10; 2 Thess. 3:3

103—GOD MOVES IN A MYSTERIOUS WAY
God's care and guidance; we trust in his ways and methods although we do not always understand.

Rom. 11:33
2 Sam. 22:7-20; Job 28; Prov. 21:30; Eccl. 3:11; Isa. 40:28; Jer. 17:7; Dan. 2:22; 4:35; Matt. 11:25-26; John 13:7; 2 Cor. 1:9

104—GOD OF GRACE AND GOD OF GLORY
Prayer for wisdom and courage for life, from a God of limitless grace and glory

Deut. 31:6; Ps. 84:11-12; 2 Cor. 10:4; Eph. 6:10-17; Phil. 4:13; 1 Tim. 6:12; 2 Tim. 1:7; Heb. 4:16; James 1:5

105—GOD OF OUR FATHERS
God's providential care and guidance of the nation; praise; patriotism; security in God

Exod. 3:15; Ps. 33:12; 44:1-3, 8; 77:14; 147:12-15; Prov. 14:34; 29:18; Isa. 40:26; 63:16; 1 Tim. 2:1-2

106—GOD, THAT MADEST EARTH AND HEAVEN
Evening; prayer for God's presence and guidance

Ps. 3:5; 42:8; 91:11-12; 104:20-24; 121:7; 139:18; John 9:4; Rom. 13:12; 1 Thess. 5:9-10; 1 Pet. 1:14

107—GOD THE ALMIGHTY ONE or GOD THE OMNIPOTENT
Praise; prayer for peace; where men fail, Almighty God's love, mercy, and power remain faithful and just.

2 Sam. 22:7-18; Job 37:2-5; Ps. 24:8; 29:10-11; 33:4; 36:5; 37:28; 97:2; 103:9-17; 116:5; 138:2; Prov. 16:6; Jer. 12:1; Nah. 1:3; John 5:39; 1 Tim. 1:2

108—GOD WHO TOUCHEST EARTH WITH BEAUTY
Christian life; prayer expressing desire for purity, joy, strength, righteousness, and a new creation of life from God

Ps. 86:5; Ezek. 16:14; 36:26-27; Hos. 12:6; Phil. 4:8; 1 Pet. 1:22-23;

1 John 4:7-21
St. 1—John 3:6; 2 Cor. 5:17
St. 2—Ps. 18:1-2; 65:3
St. 3—Ps. 4:7; 24:5; Rom. 15:13
St. 4—Heb. 6:10; 1 John 4:7
St. 5—John 14:15-18; Jude 24

109—GOD WILL TAKE CARE OF YOU
We can depend on God's providential care.

Deut. 31:8; Josh. 1:9; Ps. 55:22; 57:1; 91:11; Isa. 41:10; Luke 12:6-7; Phil. 4:19; 1 Pet. 5:7

110—GOOD CHRISTIAN MEN, REJOICE
Birth of Christ; joy; purpose for his coming

Luke 1:77-79; 2:10-20; Eph. 1:3-12

111—GRACE GREATER THAN OUR SIN
God's wonderful grace cleanses and pardons all our sin.

Rom. 3:24-26; 5:20; 6:14; Eph. 1:6-8; 2:4-9; Titus 2:11; 3:5-7

112—GRACIOUS SPIRIT, DWELL WITH ME
Prayer for presence of Holy Spirit; Holy Spirit as gracious, truthful, and mighty

Ps. 51:10-12; Ezek. 36:26-27; John 14:16-17; 1 Cor. 3:16; Gal. 5:25; Eph. 5:9

113—GREAT GOD, WE SING THY MIGHTY HAND
God's support, guardian care, and hope in future; New Year

Ps. 65:11; 89:13; Lam. 3:22-24; Acts 26:22; 1 Pet. 5:6

114—GREAT IS THY FAITHFULNESS
God's faithfulness, love, and mercy to us

Lam. 3:22-23; James 1:17
Deut. 4:31; 7:9; 1 Chron. 16:23; Ps. 9:10; 36:5-7; 89:1-2; 102:11-12
St. 2—Ps. 19:1-10; 57:10
St. 3—1 Cor. 1:4-9; 2 Tim. 2:13

115—GUIDE ME, O THOU GREAT JEHOVAH
God's presence, guidance, and care; God as our refuge

Ps. 23; 48:14; 73:24; 78:52; John 4:14; Phil. 4:19
St. 1—Exod. 16:4-18; Deut. 9:29; Ps. 78:52; 139:10; John 6:48-51;
    Heb. 11:13
St. 2—Exod. 13:21-22; Neh. 9:19-20; Ps. 28:7; 78:15-16; Zech. 13:1;
    1 Cor. 10:3-4; Rev. 22:1-2
St. 3—Josh. 3:1-17; Ps. 27:4-7; 34:1-4; Rev. 7:9-17

116—HAIL, THOU ONCE DESPISED JESUS
Praise of Christ as King; forgiveness; atonement; blood of Christ

Isa. 53:3-6; Luke 24:26; Gal. 3:13; Phil. 2:5-11; Heb. 2:9-10; 12:2; Rev.
1:5-6; 5:6-14
St. 2—John 1:29; Eph. 1:7; 2:13; 1 Pet. 1:18-19; 1 John 4:9-10
St. 4—1 Tim. 6:15-16

117—HAIL TO THE LORD'S ANOINTED
Advent; praise at the coming of Christ

Ps. 72—paraphrase
Isa. 9:6-7; Zech. 13:1; Matt. 11:3; 21:9; Luke 1:31-33; John 1:29

HALLELUJAH, WHAT A SAVIOR—See "MAN OF SORROWS"

118—HAPPY THE HOME WHEN GOD IS THERE
Happiness of a Christian home

Josh. 24:15; Prov. 22:6; Mark 10:7-9; Luke 19:9; Eph. 5:21-33; 6:1-4;
Col. 3:18-21; 1 Tim. 5:8

119—HARK! TEN THOUSAND HARPS
Christ as King; return of Christ; glory of Christ; adoration and praise;
love of Christ

Rev. 22:3-5
Isa. 60:19; Rom. 8:35-39; Heb. 2:7-10; 1 Pet. 3:22

120—HARK! THE HERALD ANGELS SING
Birth of Christ—join the angels in praise; purpose of Christ's coming

Isa. 9:6; Mic. 5:2; Luke 2:13-14; Heb. 1:6
St. 1—Luke 2:11, 13-14; 2 Cor. 5:19
St. 2—Isa. 7:14; Matt. 1:22-23; Luke 1:33-35; John 1:14
St. 3—Mal. 4:2; Matt. 20:28; Luke 1:77-79; John 3:3-17; 8:12;
       10:10; Gal. 4:4-6

121—HARK, THE VOICE OF JESUS CALLING
Expression of commitment to serve God by doing our part as much as we are able

Isa. 6:8
Matt. 9:37-38; 25:34-40; Luke 10:2; John 12:26; 21:15-17; Col. 3:24

122—HAVE THINE OWN WAY, LORD
Personal expression of submission to the will of God

Isa. 64:8; Rom. 6:13; 12:1-2; Heb. 13:21
St. 1—Isa. 64:8; Rom. 9:21
St. 2—Ps. 26:2; 51:7
St. 3—Ps. 147:3; James 5:15
St. 4—1 Cor. 6:20; Gal. 2:20

123—HE HIDETH MY SOUL
Expression of confidence in fellowship with God by redemption

Exod. 33:22
Ps. 49:15; Rom. 8:32; 1 Cor. 15:57; Eph. 1:3; 2 Tim. 1:12; 1 John 4:14

124—HE KEEPS ME SINGING
Presence of Christ in our lives gives us a song in our heart

Isa. 41:10; John 14:27; 2 Cor. 2:4; Eph. 5:19
St. 1—John 14:27
St. 2—2 Cor. 5:17
St. 3—Ps. 57:1; 2 Tim. 2:1
St. 4—John 16:33
St. 5—Luke 21:27; Col. 3:4
Refrain—Phil. 2:9

125—HE LEADETH ME, O BLESSED THOUGHT
Communion with God; God's guidance and care

Ps. 23; 48:14; 73:23-24; 139:10, 24; Isa. 41:13-14; 48:17; Luke 1:78-79; John 16:13

126—HE LIVES
Christ lives today.

Job 19:25; John 14:19; Rom. 6:9; Phil. 3:10; 1 Pet. 1:3; Rev. 1:18

St. 2—Titus 2:13
St. 3—John 16:22; Phil. 3:1
Refrain—Eph. 3:17

127—HE WHO WOULD VALIANT BE
We follow Christ and depend on him in our Christian pilgrimage.

Josh. 23:6; Ps. 108:13; 1 Cor. 15:58; 2 Cor. 10:4; Col. 3:24; 1 Tim.
6:12; 1 John 5:4

128—HEAVENLY SUNLIGHT
Jesus is our light; we walk in his light.

Prov. 4:18; John 1:4-5; 8:12; 12:46; Eph. 5:8; Rev. 21:23-24

129—HERE, O MY LORD, I SEE THEE
Lord's Supper

Matt. 26:26-29; 1 Cor. 10:16-22; 11:23-28; 2 Cor. 4:18; Rev. 19:9

130—HIGHER GROUND
Testimony of our desire and effort to press on to new heights in
Christian experience

1 Cor. 9:24; Phil. 3:13-14; Heb. 12:1-2

131—HOLY GOD, WE PRAISE THY NAME
All earth and heaven throughout the ages give praise to God; Trinity

Ps. 30:4; 145:21; Isa. 6:3; Heb. 1:8; 1 Pet. 2:9; Rev. 4:8-11; 15:4
St. 3—Eph. 2:19-20
St. 4—1 John 5:7

132—HOLY, HOLY, HOLY
Worship; morning; Trinity; daily and universal praise and adoration
to a God of power and perfection and holiness

Rev. 4:8-11
Exod. 15:11; Ps. 19:1; 62:11-12; 145:8-21; 148; Isa. 6:3; John 3:1-15;
2 Cor. 13:14; Rev. 5:13-14

133—HOLY SPIRIT, TRUTH DIVINE
Holy Spirit as truth; Holy Spirit gives light, love, and power

1 Cor. 6:19; Eph. 3:16; 2 Tim. 1:7

St. 1—John 1:1, 4-5; 14:17; 1 John 5:7
St. 2—Rom. 5:5; Gal. 5:17-18
St. 3—Acts 1:8; Eph. 3:16; Luke 24:49
St. 4—Rom. 8:1-4; 2 Cor. 3:17

134—HOLY SPIRIT (GHOST), WITH LIGHT DIVINE
Prayer that the Holy Spirit will give us light, cleansing, and joy and take complete control of our hearts

John 14:16; Rom. 8:9-11
St. 1—Eph. 5:8-9
St. 2—Luke 24:49; Titus 3:5-7
St. 3—Acts 13:52; Rom. 14:17
St. 4—John 14:17

135—HOPE OF THE WORLD
Christ as the only hope; worldwide missions

Rom. 8:24; 1 Cor. 3:11; 15:57; Col. 1:27; 1 Tim. 1:1; 1 Pet. 1:3
St. 1—Matt. 9:36
St. 2—John 6:35-51; 2 Cor. 9:15; Gal. 4:6

136—HOSANNA, LOUD HOSANNA
Palm Sunday; praise

Matt. 21:1-11; Mark 11:9-10; John 12:12-13

137—HOW FIRM A FOUNDATION
The foundations of our faith are God's Word and promises to us.

Deut. 31:6, 8; Ps. 46:1; Isa. 43:1-7; 1 Cor. 3:11; 2 Cor. 12:9; Heb. 13:5-6; 1 Pet. 2:6; 2 Pet. 1:4
St. 1—Luke 21:33
St. 2—Isa. 41:10
Last st.—John 13:23; Acts 2:27

138—HOW GREAT THOU ART
Praise and awe expressed for God's power as seen in creation and in sending his Son as Savior

Deut. 3:24; Ps. 48:1; 145:3; Rom. 1:20
St. 1 & 2—Ps. 8:3; 19:1; Acts 4:24
St. 3—Rom. 5:6; 2 Cor. 9:15
St. 4—John 14:3; 1 Thess. 4:16-17

139—HOW SWEET THE NAME OF JESUS SOUNDS
Devotion; praise and adoration of Christ; name of Christ; faith in Christ

Ps. 8:9; Matt. 12:21; Acts 4:12; Phil. 2:9-11
St. 1—John 14:27; 1 Pet. 5:7
St. 2—Matt. 11:28; John 6:51; 14:27; 1 Pet. 5:7
St. 3—Ps. 119:114; Heb. 4:16; 1 Pet. 2:7
St. 4—Matt. 21:11; John 10:27; 14:6; Heb. 2:17; Rev. 17:14

140—I AM COMING TO THE CROSS
We give our all and come to the cross for salvation and cleansing

Rom. 3:23-25; 5:8-11; 1 Cor. 1:18; Gal. 6:14; Eph. 2:16; Col. 1:20;
1 John 1:9

141—I AM THINE, O LORD
Expression of desire to be closer to Christ, his love, and his will

Ps. 16:11; 73:28; Jer. 31:3; John 10:27; Rom. 12:1-2; 1 Cor. 6:17; 7:22-24; Heb. 10:22
St. 2—Eph. 6:6; Phil. 2:13; Heb. 12:28
St. 4—John 15:11; Heb. 4:9

I CAN HEAR MY SAVIOR CALLING—See WHERE HE LEADS ME

142—I GAVE MY LIFE FOR THEE
Christ suffered and gave his life for our salvation; we are therefore indebted to him.

Ps. 116:12; Rom. 12:1-2; 1 Cor. 6:20; 7:23; 2 Cor. 5:15; 8:9; Gal. 2:20;
Phil. 2:5-11; Titus 2:14; 1 Pet. 2:21-24; 1 John 3:16

143—I HEARD THE VOICE OF JESUS SAY
Christ calls and we hear his voice and find rest, revived life, and light for our lives.

Rev. 3:20
St. 1—Matt. 11:28
St. 2—John 4:13-14
St. 3—John 1:4-5; 8:12

I HAVE FOUND A FRIEND IN JESUS—See **THE LILY OF THE VALLEY**

I KNOW NOT WHY GOD'S WONDROUS GRACE—See **I KNOW WHOM I HAVE BELIEVED**

144—I KNOW THAT MY REDEEMER LIVES
Praise and assurance that Jesus is alive

Job 19:25; Matt. 28:6; John 11:25-26; Acts 2:32; Rom. 6:9; 2 Tim. 1:10; 1 Pet. 1:3-5; Rev. 1:18
St. 2—1 Pet. 2:25
St. 3—John 15:15; Heb. 4:14
St. 4—John 14:2-3; Heb. 13:8

145—I KNOW THAT MY REDEEMER LIVETH
Return of Christ; heaven; eternal life; assurance; resurrection
Job 19:25-27
John 14:19-20; Phil. 3:20-21; 1 Thess. 1:10; Heb. 9:28; 1 Pet. 1:3-6; 2 Pet. 1:16; 1 John 2:25
St. 2—Ps. 119:89; Luke 21:33; 1 John 3:2
St. 3—John 14:2-3

146—I KNOW WHOM I HAVE BELIEVED
In the midst of many things that are a mystery to us about God, we hold to our faith.
2 Tim. 1:12
John 3:16-17; 1 Cor. 1:30-31; Eph. 1:3-10
St. 1 & 2—Rom. 5:1; Gal. 4:4-5; Eph. 2:8
St. 2—John 20:31; 1 Thess. 2:13; 2 Tim. 3:15
St. 3—John 15:26; 16:7-14
St. 4—Mark 13:35; 1 Thess. 4:16-17

147—I LAY MY SINS ON JESUS
We lay our sins and our needs on Jesus and rest in him; expression of desire to be like Jesus
Col. 2:13; 1 Tim. 2:5
St. 1—Ps. 51:2-3; Isa. 1:18; John 1:29; 1 Pet. 2:24
St. 2—2 Cor. 9:8
St. 3—Matt. 1:23; 11:28

St. 4—Matt. 11:29

148—I LOVE THY KINGDOM, LORD
Expression of praise and thanks to God for the church; supremacy of the church

Ps. 26:8; 137:5-6; Matt. 16:15-18; Eph. 5:23, 25-27; 1 Tim. 3:15

149—I LOVE TO TELL THE STORY
Soul winning; our love to God and Christ; gospel

Ps. 89:1; John 3:16-17; Acts 1:8; 4:12; 1 Tim. 1:5; Heb. 13:15; 1 Pet. 3:15; 1 John 4:9-10

150—I NEED THEE EVERY HOUR
Expression of dependence upon God and his divine companionship

Ps. 86:1-10; Act 17:27-28; Heb. 4:16
St. 1—John 16:33
St. 2—1 Cor. 10:13

151—I SING THE ALMIGHTY POWER OF GOD
We sing of the power of the God of creation.

1 Chron. 29:11-13; Ps. 33:6-8; 59:16; 95:3-6; Rev. 4:11

152—I STAND AMAZED IN THE PRESENCE
Love of Christ; suffering and death of Christ; atonement; salvation; praise and adoration

John 3:16; 15:13; Eph. 2:4-7; 3:17-19; 1 John 4:9-10
St. 1—Matt. 18:20; 1 Cor. 1:29
St. 2—Luke 22:41-44
St. 3—Luke 22:43
St. 4—Isa. 53:4-6; Matt. 8:17; 1 Pet. 3:18; 1 John 2:2
St. 5—Isa. 35:10; 1 Thess. 2:19-20; 1 Pet. 4:13

153—I SURRENDER ALL
Expression of complete submission to God

Ps. 31:5; 118:8; Matt. 22:37; John 15:4-5; Rom. 6:13; 12:1-2; 1 Cor. 6:19-20; Eph. 3:16-17; 2 Tim. 1:7

154—I WILL SING OF MY REDEEMER
Praise to Christ; love of Christ; atonement; gospel; cross of Christ

Ps. 89:1; Isa. 53:4-12; John 3:16; 1 Cor. 15:54-57; 2 Cor. 2:14; Gal. 2:20; Eph. 1:7; 2:4-6; 1 Pet. 1:18-19; 2:24; 1 John 4:9-10; Rev. 1:5*b*

155—I WILL SING THE WONDROUS STORY
Atonement; praise to Christ; cross and blood of Christ; gospel; love of Christ

Ps. 89:1; Isa. 35:10; Rom. 5:8, 11; Col. 1:11-14; 1 John 4:9-10
St. 1—John 1:14; Phil. 2:6-8
St. 2—Isa. 53:6; Matt. 18:11-14
St. 3—Luke 7:21-22; 1 Cor. 7:23-24; 1 Pet. 2:24
St. 4—John 8:12; 1 Pet. 5:7
St. 5—Ps. 23:6; Rom. 14:8

156—I'LL LIVE FOR HIM
Commitment to live for Christ, who died for us

Matt. 22:37; Mark 12:33; John 10:10-11; 11:25-26; 1 Cor. 6:20; 7:23; 2 Cor. 5:15; Gal. 2:20; Titus 2:14

I'M PRESSING ON THE UPWARD WAY—See HIGHER GROUND

157—I'VE FOUND A FRIEND
Expression of close relationship with Jesus; love of Jesus; Jesus as friend

John 15:9, 13-15; Rom. 8:35, 38-39; 12:1; Gal. 2:20; 1 John 4:13, 19

158—IF THOU BUT SUFFER GOD TO GUIDE THEE
God's eternal, providential care and guidance for those who trust in him

Ps. 55:22
2 Sam. 22:33; Ps. 28:7; 48:14; Prov. 3:5-6; Isa. 26:3-4; Phil. 4:19; 1 Pet. 5:7
St. 1—Ps. 62:2
St. 2—Matt. 6:30-32
St. 3—Ps. 9:10; 31:23

159—IMMORTAL, INVISIBLE
God as immortal, invisible, wise, almighty, and just; praise to the God of creation

1 Tim. 1:17; 6:15-16
Job 37:21-24; Ps. 27:1; 36:6; 104:1-5; Luke 10:21-22; John 1:1-14; 8:12; Rom. 16:27; 1 Cor. 8:6; 2 Cor. 4:6; 1 John 1:5; Rev. 21:23

160—IMMORTAL LOVE, FOREVER FULL
The constancy of God's immortal love

Ps. 139:7-10; Jer. 31:3; Matt. 9:20-22; Luke 6:19; Rom. 8:38-39; Eph. 3:17-19; 1 John 4:19
Last st.—John 13:13-15; Eph. 6:9

161—IN CHRIST THERE IS NO EAST OR WEST
Brotherhood; universality of Christ; oneness of fellowship in Christ
Ps. 133:1; Rom. 12:5; Gal. 3:26-28; 5:13; Col. 3:11; 1 Pet. 2:17

162—IN HEAVENLY LOVE ABIDING
Expression of faith in a consciousness of God's love
Deut. 31:8; Ps. 23; John 15:10; 2 Thess. 3:5; 1 John 4:10-18; Jude 21

163—IN LOVING KINDNESS JESUS CAME
Testimony; Jesus has lifted or redeemed our souls from sin's darkness.
Ps. 40:2; Eph. 1:3-8; 2:4-6; Col. 1:12-14; 1 Tim. 1:15; Titus 2:14; 1 Pet. 2:24-25

164—IN THE CROSS OF CHRIST I GLORY
Cross of Jesus; comfort and hope; devotion; security
Gal. 6:14
John 16:33; 19:17-18; Rom. 5:6-11; 1 Cor. 1:17-19, 23-24, 31; 2:2; Eph. 2:13; Phil. 3:3; Col. 1:20-23; Titus 2:14-15; Heb. 1:3; 1 Pet. 1:21; 2:24; 1 John 4:19

165—IN THE HOUR OF TRIAL
Expression of desire for Jesus' help and closeness in time of trial and temptation

Deut. 4:30-31; Mark 14:66-72; John 16:33; 1 Cor. 10:13
St. 2—Gal. 6:14; 1 John 2:15-16
St. 3—Ps. 55:22; 57:1; 1 Pet. 5:7

IS YOUR LIFE A CHANNEL OF BLESSING?—See **MAKE ME A BLESSING**

166—IT CAME UPON THE MIDNIGHT CLEAR
Birth of Christ; the angels' song

Luke 2:9-14
Matt. 25:31; Phil. 2:9-11; Heb. 1:6

167—IT IS WELL WITH MY SOUL
Expression of faith regardless of conditions in life

Ps. 31:14; 103:1-4; Eccl. 8:12-13; Rom. 8:28; 15:13; 2 Cor. 5:7;
Gal. 2:20; 2 Tim. 1:12; Heb. 10:22; 1 Pet. 4:19
St. 2—Heb. 2:14; 1 John 3:8
St. 3—1 Cor. 15:3; Col. 2:13-15
St. 4—Matt. 24:30-31; 1 Cor. 15:52

168—IT MAY BE AT MORN
Return of Christ; eternal life

Matt. 24:30-31, 36, 42-44; 25:13; Mark 13:32-37; Luke 12:35-40; Heb.
10:37; 2 Pet. 3:3-14; Rev. 22:20
St. 2—Matt. 24:27
St. 3—Matt. 16:27; 25:31
St. 4—Isa. 35:10; Rev. 21:4
Refrain—1 Thess. 2:19; 2 Thess. 1:10

169—JERUSALEM, MY HAPPY HOME
Immortal life; heaven viewed as the new Jerusalem

Rev. 21:2, 4
Ps. 122:2; Isa. 35:10; 65:17-19; 2 Cor. 3:18; 5:8; 1 Thess. 4:13-17; Heb.
11:16; 12:22; Rev. 21

170—JERUSALEM, THE GOLDEN
Anticipation and desire for heaven, the new Jerusalem

Isa. 35:10; Jer. 3:17; Heb. 11:16; 12:22; Rev. 7:9-17; 19:9; 21; 22
St. 1—Josh. 5:6; 1 Cor. 2:9; 2 Cor. 3:18

171—JESUS, AND SHALL IT EVER BE
Desire never to be ashamed of Jesus so that he will not be ashamed of
us

Matt. 10:33; Luke 9:26; Rom 1:16; 2 Cor. 10:17; Phil. 1:20

172—JESUS CALLS US
Jesus calls us to follow him and love him more than anything else.

Matt. 4:18-20; 4:19; 10:37-38; Luke 9:23, 57-62; John 21:15-17

173—JESUS CHRIST IS RISEN TODAY
Praise; Christ endured the cross to redeem us and is now alive and reigns as Lord and King.

Matt. 28:1-9, 18; Luke 24:6, 48; Rom. 6:9-10; 1 Cor. 15:3-4; Heb. 12:2; 1 Pet. 1:3

174—JESUS, I MY CROSS HAVE TAKEN
Expression of total commitment to Jesus' challenge to take up our crosses and follow him

Mark 10:21, 28; Luke 9:23-24; Rom. 12:1-2; 1 Pet. 2:21-24

175—JESUS IS ALL THE WORLD TO ME
Joy; adoration and devotion to Christ; Christ as Friend; expression of dependency on Christ

John 15:14-15
Isa. 26:3; John 8:12; Eph. 6:10; Phil. 4:13
St. 3—John 10:27-28; 1 Pet. 2:21
St. 4—John 10:27-28; 1 John 2:25

JESUS IS CALLING—See JESUS IS TENDERLY CALLING

JESUS IS COMING TO EARTH AGAIN—See WHAT IF IT WERE TODAY?

176—JESUS IS TENDERLY CALLING
The call or invitation of Christ

Matt. 11:28; 25:34; John 11:28; Acts 4:12; 2 Thess. 2:14; Rev. 3:20

177—JESUS, KEEP ME NEAR THE CROSS
Aspiration; cross of Christ; consecration and devotion

Zech. 13:1; John 6:47-51; 19:17-18; 1 Cor. 1:17-18; Gal. 6:14; Eph. 2:13; Col. 1:20-23; 1 Thess. 5:9-10; 1 Pet. 2:24; Rev. 5:9; 22:1, 16

178—JESUS, LOVER OF MY SOUL

Christ is our all, our refuge and our Savior; grace; calmness; love of Christ; praise of Christ

Eph. 3:16-19
Ps. 37:39; Acts 2:25; 2 Cor. 1:5; Rev. 7:17
St. 3—Ps. 147:3; Luke 7:21-22; 1 John 1:8-10
St. 4—Zech. 13:1; Rom. 5:20-21; Titus 2:11

179—JESUS, NAME OF WONDROUS LOVE

The name of Jesus

Acts 4:12; Phil. 2:9-10; Heb. 1:4; Rev. 22:4

180—JESUS PAID IT ALL

God's grace and cleansing are complete through Jesus; salvation is by grace and not by our own merit.

Isa. 1:18; Rom. 3:24-26; 5:6; 1 Cor. 6:11; Eph. 1:7-9; Titus 3:5-6; 1 Pet. 2:22-25
St. 2—Matt. 8:2-3
St. 3—Isa. 1:18
St. 4—Rev. 7:14-15

JESUS SAVES—See WE HAVE HEARD A JOYFUL SOUND

181—JESUS SAVIOR, PILOT ME

Jesus guides us in life as a pilot guides a ship at sea.

Ps. 89:9; 107:28-30; Matt. 8:23-27; Luke 8:24-25; James 1:6

182—JESUS SHALL REIGN

Christ as King; exaltation of Christ

Ps. 72
Ps. 67; Luke 1:32-33; 22:69; 1 Cor. 15:27; Phil. 2:9-11; Col. 1:17-19; Heb. 1:8; Rev. 5:12-13; 7:9-10; 11:15
St. 1—Ps. 72:5, 8, 17
St. 2—Ps. 72:10-14
St. 3—Ps. 72:11, 15
St. 4—Ps. 72:15, 17; Matt. 21:16; Col. 3:16

183—JESUS, THE VERY THOUGHT OF THEE
Praise and love for Christ; name of Christ; joy; devotion

Matt. 12:21; Luke 1:47; John 16:33; Acts 2:28; 1 Thess. 2:19-20
St. 1—1 Cor. 13:12; Eph. 3:17
St. 2—Ps. 66:2; Acts 4:12; Phil. 2:9-11
St. 3—Ps. 130:7; Jer. 17:7; Rom. 15:13; 1 Pet. 1:21
St. 4—John 15:9; Eph. 3:19; 1 John 3:1, 16

184—JESUS, THOU JOY OF LOVING HEARTS
Praise to Christ; devotion; prayer; joy; aspiration

Luke 1:47; John 14:1; 15:10-11; Eph. 3:17; 2 Pet. 1:3
St. 1—John 6:35; 1 Cor. 1:9; Phil. 4:19; Rev. 7:17
St. 2—Ps. 100:5; 1 Cor. 1:9
St. 3—Heb. 11:6; 1 Pet. 1:8-9
St. 4—Matt. 28:20; John 1:4-5; Col. 1:13

185—JESUS, THY BLOOD AND RIGHTEOUSNESS
Atonement; blood of Jesus

Isa. 61:10; Rom. 3:24-25; 5:8-11; 1 Tim. 2:5-6; 1 Pet. 1:18-19; Rev. 7:14

186—JESUS, THY BOUNDLESS LOVE TO ME
Commitment to a Christ of limitless love; through love of Jesus, we receive peace, power, comfort, and eternal life.

John 15:9-10; Rom. 8:35-39; Gal. 2:20; Eph. 2:4-5; 3:17-19; 2 Tim. 1:7; 1 John 3:1

187—JESUS, WHAT A FRIEND FOR SINNERS
Commitment to Jesus as friend, our strength, comfort, guide, and our all

John 15:13-15; Eph. 3:19
St. 2—2 Cor. 12:9
St. 3—John 14:18; 2 Cor. 1:5
St. 4—Ps. 107:28-30; Matt. 8:23-27
St. 5—Song of Sol. 2:16; John 1:12

188—JESUS, WITH THY CHURCH ABIDE
Expression of our desire for the presence of Christ in the church's worship, fellowship, and work

Matt. 16:15-18; Acts 4:32; Rom. 8:9; 12:4-5; Eph. 1:22-23; 2:19-22; Col. 1:18

189—JOY TO THE WORLD
Birth of Christ; praise for God's redemption

Ps. 98; Luke 2:11
Gen. 3:17-18; Luke 1:46-55; Rom. 5:20

190—JOYFUL, JOYFUL, WE ADORE THEE
Praise and adoration of a God of majesty and power; joy of living in God's world

Ps. 98; Hab. 3:18-19; Luke 19:38; 1 John 1:7
St. 1—John 10:10*b*; 12:46; James 1:17
St. 2—Ps. 19:1; 145:10; 148
St. 3—Ps. 103:3-5; 1 Pet. 2:17; 3:8
St. 4—Job 38:7; 1 Cor. 15:57; 2 Cor. 2:14; Col. 2:2

191—JUDGE ETERNAL, THRONED IN SPLENDOR
Prayer to an omnipotent God for help; God as judge

1 Chron. 29:11; Ps. 58:11; 75:7; Isa. 33:22; Heb. 1:8
St. 1—Deut. 10:17; Ps. 79:9; Mal. 4:2
Last st.—John 15:13; Eph. 5:26; 6:17

192—JUST AS I AM, THINE OWN TO BE
Expression of commitment of our complete selves to Christ; purpose for living

Ps. 71:5; Rom. 6:13; 12:1-2; 1 Cor. 6:20; Eph. 5:8; 6:10; 1 Tim. 4:12

193—JUST AS I AM, WITHOUT ONE PLEA
We come to Jesus as we are for cleansing and pardon; all barriers are broken down.

Ps. 51:1-2; Isa. 1:18; John 6:37; 1 Cor. 1:9; Eph. 2:13; Col. 1:14; 1 John 1:7-9; Rev. 22:17

194—LAMP OF OUR FEET, WHEREBY WE TRACE
Word of God as a lamp and guide in life

Deut. 8:3; Ps. 119:128-130; Matt. 4:4; Luke 11:28; 24:45; 2 Tim. 3:15-16; 2 Pet. 1:19

195—LEAD KINDLY LIGHT
God's presence, comfort, guidance, and leadership; God as a light in a world of darkness

Ps. 43:3
Ps. 32:8; 36:9; 73:24; Dan. 2:22; John 3:19-21; 8:12; 12:35-36, 46; Acts 26:18; Rom. 12:2

196—LEAD ME TO CALVARY
Remembrance of events of Gethsemane and Calvary and of God's love

Luke 23:33; 24:26; John 19:17; 1 Cor. 15:3; Gal. 2:20; 6:14;
Heb. 12:2-3
St. 1—John 19:2
St. 2—John 19:38-42
St. 3—Luke 24:1-9
St. 4—Matt. 10:38; 20:22

197—LEAD ON, O KING ETERNAL
Challenge to follow Christ in spiritual warfare

Isa. 48:17; Eph. 6:10-20; Phil. 1:27-30; 1 Tim. 6:12; 2 Tim. 2:3-4; 4:7-8;
Jude 3; Rev. 17:14
St. 1—2 Cor. 12:9
St. 2—1 Cor. 15:56-58
St. 3—Gal. 6:14; 2 Tim. 4:8

198—LEAD US, O FATHER, IN THE PATHS OF PEACE
Prayer for God's guidance and leadership in the path of life

Ps. 25:4, 10; 37:23; 48:14; Prov. 3:6; Jer. 10:23; Hos. 14:9
St. 1—Luke 1:79; John 14:6; 16:33
St. 2—Ps. 86:11
St. 3—Prov. 3:23; 4:11
St. 4—Eph. 4:13; Heb. 4:9; Rev. 14:13

199—LEANING ON THE EVERLASTING ARMS
Fellowship with Jesus gives peace; Christ as our refuge on our pilgrimage in life

Deut. 33:27; Ps. 118:6; Prov. 3:23; 1 Cor. 1:9

200—LET ALL MORTAL FLESH KEEP SILENCE
God comes to earth; all earth and heaven give praise.

Ps. 5:7; 89:5-7; Isa. 6:3; Hab. 2:20; Zech. 2:13; Luke 1:77-79; John 1:4-5, 14; Rev. 4:8-11

201—LET ALL THE WORLD IN EVERY CORNER SING
Individuals, church, everyone, and everything praise God.

Ps. 47:6; 66:4; 67:3-5; 69:34; 145:21; 150:6; Heb. 2:12; 13:15; Rev. 5:13

202—LET US BREAK BREAD TOGETHER
Lord's Supper; praise; prayer for mercy

Matt. 26:26-30; Luke 24:30; John 6:53-58; 1 Cor. 11:23-28

203—LET US WITH A GLADSOME MIND
Praise to God for his eternal kindness and mercy

Ps. 136:1-2, 7, 25-26—paraphrase
Ps. 63:3; 89:1; 100:5; 106:1; 107:8-9; 136; 145:9; James 1:17

204—LIFT UP YOUR HEADS
Anticipation of Christ's coming

Ps. 24:7-10
Luke 21:28; James 5:8; 2 Cor. 4:6

205—LIVING FOR JESUS
Commitment to live a life totally committed to Jesus

Mark 12:33; Luke 9:23-24; Rom. 6:13, 18; 12:1-2; 1 Cor. 6:20; 7:23; 2 Cor. 4:10-11; Gal. 2:20; Col. 1:10; Titus 2:14; 1 Pet. 2:21, 24; 1 John 5:11-12

206—LO, HE COMES WITH CLOUDS DESCENDING
Return and reign of Christ; praise; resurrection

1 Thess. 4:16-17
Dan. 7:13-14; Matt. 16:27-28; 25:31-46; Mark 13:26-27; 14:62; Luke 21:27-28, 31; Acts 1:9-11; 2 Thess. 1:7-10; Heb. 9:28; 2 Pet. 3:3-14; Rev. 1:7-8
St. 4—Zech. 14:9; Luke 1:33

207—LOOK, YE SAINTS
Christ as Savior, King, and Lord; adoration of Jesus

Matt. 25:31; Acts 2:36; Phil. 2:9-11; Heb. 2:7-10; 12:2; Rev. 11:15
St. 2—1 Pet. 3:22
St. 3—Matt. 20:19; John 5:31

208—LORD, DISMISS US WITH THY BLESSING
Prayer for God's joy, peace, and blessings; worship; evening; benediction

Heb. 13:20-21
St. 1—Num. 6:24; Gal. 6:16; Eph. 6:23-24; Phil. 1:2
St. 2—Rom. 15:13; 1 Tim. 2:1-2; Heb. 6:9; 2 Pet. 1:2
St. 3—Ps. 23:4; Prov. 14:32; Luke 20:36; 1 Thess. 4:13-18

LORD JESUS, I LONG TO BE—See WHITER THAN SNOW

209—LORD JESUS, THINK ON ME
Desire that Jesus would "think on me"; prayer for cleansing from sin; in earthly problems, we look to the eternal rest that is promised.

Ps. 25:7; 40:17; 106:4; Luke 23:42-43; Heb. 4:9

210—LORD OF ALL BEING
God as light and flame, star and sun, and center of all being

2 Sam. 22:29; Ps. 36:9; 84:11; 104:2; Isa. 60:1, 19-20; Acts 17:28; 2 Cor. 4:6; James 1:17

211—LORD OF OUR LIFE
Prayer for peace and victory over earthly foes

Ps. 25:1-5; 27:1; 29:11; 79:9; Isa. 26:3; John 16:33

212—LORD, SPEAK TO ME
We follow Jesus' example and leading in service.

2 Tim. 2:2
Ps. 119:12-13; Matt. 28:19-20; John 13:15; Acts 1:8; Rom. 6:13; 12:1-2
St. 4—1 John 2:17

213—LORD, THY WORD ABIDETH
God's Word dwells in us to guide and strengthen us.

Ps. 19:7-8; 119:105, 128-130; Luke 11:28; 1 Thess. 2:13; 2 Tim. 3:15-17; 2 Pet. 1:19-21

214—LOVE DIVINE, ALL LOVES EXCELLING
God's love, mercy, and salvation; worship and praise; Advent

1 John 4:7-21
John 14:21; 1 John 3:1; 3:16
St. 1—Ps. 106:4; John 14:16-17; Col. 2:9-10; Rev. 21:3
St. 2—Matt. 11:28-29; John 20:22; 2 Cor. 3:18; Gal. 5:1; Col. 3:11; Heb. 4:3-11; Rev. 1:8
St. 3—Ps. 138; 1-5; 2 Pet. 2:9; Rev. 7:15
St. 4—2 Cor. 5:17; 2 Pet. 3:13-14; Jude 24-25; Rev. 7:15

LOW IN THE GRAVE HE LAY—See CHRIST AROSE

215—MAJESTIC SWEETNESS SITS ENTHRONED
Reign and lordship of Christ; exaltation of Christ; eternal life; atonement; Christ as Savior; praise

Col. 1:15-20; Heb. 1:3
Song of Sol. 5:10-16; John 17:1-5; Acts 5:30-31; Rom. 14:9; 1 Cor. 15:54-58; Phil. 2:8-11; Rev. 5:12-13
St. 1—Luke 22:69
St. 2—John 8:51-56
St. 3 & 4—Acts 2:24-28; Gal. 2:20; Eph. 2:4-5

216—MAKE ME A BLESSING and MAKE ME A CHANNEL OF BLESSING
Prayer that God will use us and our lives as ambassadors for Christ, telling others of his love for us and for them

Isa. 6:8; Matt. 4:19; 5:16; Luke 14:23; John 13:35; 15:4-8; 21:15-17; Acts 20:24; 2 Tim. 2:21

217—"MAN OF SORROWS," WHAT A NAME
Suffering and death of Christ; cross; Christ as Savior; name of Christ; praise and adoration of Christ

1 John 4:14
Isa. 53:3-6; Mark 10:45; Phil. 2:7-11; 1 Pet. 2:24
St. 2—John 19:1-3; Col. 1:20; Heb. 13:12
St. 3—John 19:30; Heb. 12:2

St. 4—Isa. 35:10; John 14:2-3

MARVELOUS GRACE OF OUR LOVING LORD—See **GRACE GREATER THAN OUR SIN**

MASTER OF EAGER YOUTH—See **SHEPHERD OF TENDER YOUTH**

218—MOMENT BY MOMENT
We belong to God and are kept in his love and are given life from above.

Ps. 116:1-9; John 16:33; 2 Cor. 12:9; Gal. 2:19-20; Eph. 3:17; 1 Pet. 1:5; 5:7

219—MORE ABOUT JESUS
Desire expressed to know more about Jesus, his Word, and his will

Eph. 3:19; 4:13-15; Phil. 3:8; Col. 1:9; 1 Pet. 2:2; 3:18; 1 John 2:27
St. 2—John 14:26
St. 3—John 5:39

220—MORE LOVE TO THEE, O CHRIST
Expression of desire to show more love to Christ

Phil. 1:9; 2 Thess. 3:5; 1 John 4:19

221—MUST JESUS BEAR THE CROSS ALONE
As servants of God, we bear our own crosses and persevere until we go home for our reward.

Matt. 16:24-27; 19:27-28; Phil. 1:21; 3:10; Heb. 3:14
St. 2 & 3—Luke 21:19; Rev. 14:12-13

222—MY FAITH LOOKS UP TO THEE
Expression of the confidence we can have in our faith in Christ

Ps. 118:8; Rom. 1:17; 5:1-2; Eph. 3:12; Heb. 12:2; Rev. 7:17
St. 1—John 1:29
St. 2—2 Cor. 12:9; 1 John 4:19
St. 3—Ps. 73:24; Isa. 51:11
St. 4—John 14:1-3

MY FATHER IS RICH—See **A CHILD OF THE KING**

MY HOPE IS BUILT—See **THE SOLID ROCK**

223—MY JESUS, AS THOU WILT
Expression of submission to will of God no matter what the future may bring

Ps. 40:8; Matt. 6:10; Mark 14:36; Rom. 12:2; Eph. 5:17; 6:6; Heb. 13:21; James 4:15; 1 John 2:17

MY LIFE, MY LOVE I GIVE—See **I'LL LIVE FOR HIM**

MY REDEEMER—See **I WILL SING OF MY REDEEMER**

MY SAVIOR'S LOVE—See **I STAND AMAZED IN THE PRESENCE**

224—MY JESUS, I LOVE THEE
Expression of love and gratitude for Jesus and what he has done for us

Matt. 22:37; 1 Pet. 1:8; 2:9; 1 John 4:19
St. 4—John 14:2-3

225—MY SOUL, BE ON THY GUARD
Steadfastness in spiritual warfare until victory and crown are won

Matt. 26:41; 1 Cor. 15:58; 16:13; Eph. 6:10-20; Phil. 1:27-30; 1 Tim. 6:12; 2 Tim. 2:3-4; 4:7-8; Heb. 10:23; 1 Pet. 5:8-9; 2 Pet. 3:17

NEAR THE CROSS—See **JESUS, KEEP ME NEAR THE CROSS**

226—NEAR TO THE HEART OF GOD
Expression of faith; rest, comfort, and peace come in closeness to God

Exod. 33:14; Ps. 34:18; 73:28; Matt. 11:28-30; Acts 17:27; Phil. 4:7; Heb. 4:16; James 4:8

227—NEARER, MY GOD, TO THEE
Prayer of devotion expressing desire for closer fellowship with God

Ps. 16:8; 73:28; 145:18; Acts 17:27
St. 3 & 4—Gen. 28:10-22
St. 4—Gen. 35:15

228—NO, NOT ONE
Jesus is always near to help us in all needs of life.

Prov. 18:24; John 15:13-15; Eph. 1:3
St. 2—Matt. 11:29; Phil. 2:5-9
St. 3—John 8:12
St. 4—John 6:37; Rev. 3:20
St. 5—2 Cor. 5:1; 9:15

229—NOTHING BUT THE BLOOD
Atonement; blood of Jesus cleanses and pardons

Isa. 1:18; Zech. 13:1; Rom. 3:24-25; Eph. 1:7; Col. 1:14; Heb. 9:14, 22; 1 Pet. 1:18-19; Rev. 7:14

230—NOW THANK WE ALL OUR GOD
Thanksgiving; thanks expressed to an omnipotent God for all his blessings

1 Chron. 16:8, 34-36; 29:13; Ps. 75:1; 92:1; 140:13; Col. 1:12; 1 Thess. 5:18; Heb. 13:15; Rev. 11:17

231—NOW THE DAY IS OVER
Worship; benediction; evening; care of God

Gen. 1:4-5; Ps. 3:5; 4:8; 63:6-8; 91:5, 11; 104:19-23; 139:11; Prov. 3:24-25

232—O BROTHER MAN
Brotherhood; oneness in Christ in service, love, and worship

Ps. 133:1; Matt. 25:40; John 15:12; Rom. 15:1-2; Gal. 5:13; 6:10; Phil. 2:1-2; 1 Pet. 1:22; 3:8; 1 John 4:11, 21

O CHRISTIAN HASTE—See O ZION HASTE

233—O COME, ALL YE FAITHFUL
Birth of Christ; shepherds, angels; invitation to join in praise and adoration of Christ

Luke 2:15
St. 1—Matt. 2:2; Luke 2:15
St. 2—Luke 2:9-14
St. 3—Luke 1:68-69; John 1:1, 14

234—O COME, O COME, EMMANUEL
Anticipation of the coming of Jesus to earth; Advent

Isa. 7:14; Matt. 1:23; Rev. 22:20
St. 2—Isa. 11:1; Zech. 13:1
St. 3—Luke 1:78-79
St. 4—Isa. 22:22; Rev. 3:7-8

235—O COULD I SPEAK THE MATCHLESS WORTH
Atonement; Christ as Savior, Friend, and Lord; love of Christ; blood of Christ; return of Christ; grace; joy; adoration

Isa. 35:10; 1 Cor. 13:12; Heb. 1:3; 2:9-12; Jude 24-25; Rev. 1:5-6; 5:9-13; 22:3-5

236—O DAY OF REST AND GLADNESS
Lord's Day; worship and praise; Trinity compared to a threefold sabbath: (*a*) creation of light; (*b*) resurrection of Christ; (*c*) Holy Spirit sent from heaven

Gen. 1:3-5; Ps. 118:24; Isa. 58:13-14; 66:23; Rev. 1:10
St. 1—Gen. 1:3-5; 2:2-3; Isa. 6:3
St. 2—Gen. 1:3-5; Mark 16:9; John 20:1*a*, 19*a*, 21-22
St. 3—Isa. 56:2, 6-7; Mark 2:27
St. 4—Heb. 4:9-11

237—O FOR A CLOSER WALK WITH GOD
Expression of desire to walk close to God; confession of sin and repentance from sin and worship of false idols

Gen. 5:24; Ps. 34:18; 56:13; Prov. 4:18; Isa. 55:6-7; Mic. 6:8; Acts 17:27-30; Gal. 5:16; Eph. 5:8

238—O FOR A FAITH THAT WILL NOT SHRINK
Expression of faith in the various situations of life

Ps. 27; 71:1; Mark 9:23-24; 11:22; Luke 17:5-6; 1 Cor. 16:13; 2 Cor. 5:7; Eph. 6:16; 1 John 5:4
St. 4—John 11:40

239—O FOR A HEART TO PRAISE MY GOD
Expression of desire for a heart characterized by holiness, humility, renewal, and love

Deut. 5:29; 1 Kings 8:61; Ps. 9:1; 51:10; Jer. 24:7; Mic. 6:8; James 4:8, 10; 1 Pet. 3:15

240—O FOR A THOUSAND TONGUES TO SING
Praise; Christ as Savior and Lord; blood of Christ; name of Christ

Ps. 96:1-4; 103:1-4; 1 Cor. 1:31; Phil. 2:9-11; Rev. 5:12
St. 1—Ps. 71:23
St. 2—Isa. 12:4-5; Matt. 12:21
St. 3—Matt. 12:21; 2 Cor. 1:3-7; 1 Pet. 5:7
St. 4—Isa. 1:18; John 8:34-36; Rom. 3:24-25; Eph. 1:7

241—O GOD, OUR HELP IN AGES PAST
Majesty of God; prayer for God's presence and power in our lives and our nation

Ps. 90:1-4
Ps. 33:20; 38:15; 46:1; Isa. 26:4
St. 2—Ps. 91:1-2
St. 3—Ps. 90:2; Lam. 5:19
St. 4—Ps. 90:4; 2 Pet. 3:8
St. 5—Ps. 48:14

242—O HAPPY DAY THAT FIXED MY CHOICE
Conversion described as "a choice, bond, great transaction, and rest for a long-divided heart"; joy in redemption

2 Chron. 15:15; Ps. 32:11; Isa. 61:10; Luke 10:20; Eph. 1:7; Phil. 4:4; Col. 1:20-21; Titus 3:5-6; 1 John 1:8-9

243—O HAPPY HOME, WHERE THOU ART LOVED
Happiness of a home in which Christ is central

Josh. 24:15; Mark 10:7-9; Luke 19:9; Eph. 5:21-33; 6:1-4; Col. 3:18-21; 1 Tim. 5:8

244—O HOW I LOVE JESUS
Name of Jesus; blood of Jesus; expression of love for God and Jesus

Ps. 66:2; Matt. 12:21; Acts 4:12; Phil. 2:9-11; Heb. 1:4

St. 2—Rom 6:2-11; Col. 1:13-14; 1 John 4:9-10; Rev. 1:5
St. 3—John 8:12; Col. 1:13
St. 4—2 Cor. 1:3-7; Heb. 4:15-16; 1 Pet. 5:7
Refrain—1 John 4:19

245—O JESUS, I HAVE PROMISED

Prayer of complete discipleship, looking to God for strength and guidance

Luke 9:23-24, 57-62; John 12:26; 15:14; 21:15-17; Rom. 12:11; Col. 3:24; 1 Tim. 1:12; Rev. 14:13

246—O JESUS, THOU ART STANDING

Jesus stands, knocks, and pleads at the doors of our hearts.

Rev. 3:20
John 10:1-9; 14:6; Rev. 22:17

247—O LITTLE TOWN OF BETHLEHEM

Birth of Jesus; he enters the world as prophesied; born to save; prayer that he would be born again in us

Mic. 5:2
Matt. 2:1-12; Luke 2:1-7
St. 1—Isa. 9:2; Luke 2:11; John 1:9
St. 2—Job 38:7; Luke 1:26-38
St. 3—John 3:16
St. 4—Isa. 7:14; Matt. 1:23; 2 Cor. 6:16

O LORD, MY GOD—See HOW GREAT THOU ART

248—O LOVE, THAT WILT NOT LET ME GO

The Christian's cross brings him the fullness of God's love, light, and joy.

Jer. 31:3; John 12:32; 15:9-11
St. 1—Rom. 8:35-39; Eph. 3:17-19
St. 2—2 Sam. 22:29; Ps. 36:9; John 8:12
St. 3—Rom. 15:13
St. 4—Matt. 16:24; Gal. 6:14

249—O MASTER, LET ME WALK WITH THEE

Prayer to be more like Christ in character and service to men; desire for companionship with the Master

Matt. 4:19; Luke 6:40; John 12:26; 13:13-14; Gal. 5:13; Col. 1:10; 1 John 2:6
St. 2—John 13:35
St. 3—Luke 21:19; Rev. 14:12

250—O PERFECT LOVE
Marriage; wedding prayer

Eph. 5:31
Gen. 2:18, 23-24; Josh. 24:15; Mark 10:7-9; Eph. 5:21-33; 1 Pet. 3:7

251—O SACRED HEAD, NOW WOUNDED
Prayer of thanks and expression of devotion to Christ for his suffering and death in our place

Isa. 53
Isa. 63:9; Luke 24:26; Phil. 2:8; Heb. 2:9; 5:8; 1 Pet. 3:18
St. 1—Isa. 53:3; Matt. 27:26-50; John 19:2
St. 2—Isa. 53:5; John 10:11; Rom. 5:6-8; 1 Pet. 2:24
St. 3—1 Cor. 15:57; 16:22; 2 Cor. 5:14; 1 John 4:19

252—O SONS AND DAUGHTERS
Christ's resurrection; praise; women and angels at empty tomb

Matt. 28:1-9; Luke 24:6; John 20:29; 2 Cor. 6:18; 1 Pet. 1:3

253—O THAT WILL BE GLORY
Immortal life; anticipation of heaven

Isa. 35:10; John 14:2-4; Acts 20:32; 1 Cor. 13:12; 2 Cor. 3:18; 5:8; Col. 3:4; Heb. 4:9; 1 John 2:25; 3:2; Rev. 14:13

254—O WHERE ARE KINGS AND EMPIRES NOW?
The church as built on the foundation of Jesus Christ stands after years of struggle.

Ps. 46; Dan. 2:35-44; Matt. 16:15-18; 1 Cor. 3:11; Col. 1:18

255—O WORD OF GOD INCARNATE
Incarnate Word; God's Word as guide in life; church's role in transmitting the word

Ps. 60:4; 119:105, 160; Isa. 40:8; Mark 13:31; (*see next page*)

John 1:1-5, 14; 5:39; 2 Pet. 1:19; Rev. 1:3

256—O WORSHIP THE KING
Worship; praise and adoration to Christ as King; trust in the infinite God, our Creator

Ps. 104
Ps. 22:28-31; 47:6-7; 71:6-8; 145:1-13; 1 Tim. 6:15-16
St. 1—1 Chron. 29:11-13; Ps. 104:1a; 138:2
St. 2—Ps. 21:13; 104:1-4; Jer. 33:11
St. 3—Job 37:9-13; Ps. 104:5-28
St. 4—Ps. 13:5; 46:1; 52:8-9; 78:29-35; Isa. 2:22

257—O ZION HASTE
Missions; a call to Christians to the challenge of bringing the message of Christ to the world

Ps. 67:2; Isa. 52:7; 61:1; Luke 24:47; John 1:4-10; 3:15-17; 17:18; Acts 1:8; Rom. 10:15
St. 1—Matt. 18:14; 2 Pet. 3:9; 1 John 1:5
St. 2—Prov. 11:7
St. 3—Acts 17:28; 1 John 4:9-10
St. 4—Amos 2:11; Matt. 25:23

258—OF THE FATHER'S LOVE BEGOTTEN
Eternal existence of Christ; Christ as first and last; birth of Christ
John 1:1, 14; Phil. 2:7-11; Heb. 13:8; Rev. 1:8, 18

ON A HILL FAR AWAY—See THE OLD RUGGED CROSS

259—ON JORDAN'S STORMY BANKS
Anticipation of heaven compared with Israel's anticipation of the promised land
Num. 14:8; Deut. 4:22; Isa. 35:10; 2 Cor. 5:8; Heb. 11:16; 1 John 2:25; 3:2; Rev. 14:13; 21:4

260—ONCE IN ROYAL DAVID'S CITY
Jesus' birth, childhood, and example to us; humanity of Jesus
Luke 2:4-7, 11-12, 40, 52; 2 Cor. 8:9; Phil. 2:5-11

261—ONCE TO EVERY MAN AND NATION

A challenge to stand by Christian truth and principles in the face of evil

Deut. 30:15; Josh. 24:15; Ps. 84:10; Luke 16:13; Rom. 12:9, 21; 2 Cor. 13:7-8; Eph. 6:13-17; 1 Thess. 5:21-22; 1 Pet. 3:8-12

262—ONE DAY

Christ: birth, death, resurrection, and Second Coming; atonement; cross; Savior

Luke 24:46; John 3:13-17; Acts 17:3; Rom. 4:25; 2 Cor. 9:15; Eph. 5:2; Phil. 2:5-11; 1 Thess. 5:10; 1 Tim. 3:16; Heb. 1:3; 9:28; 12:2
St. 1—Matt. 1:22-23; Luke 2:13-14; John 1:14; 1 John 2:6
St. 2—Isa. 53; Mark 15:15-39; John 12:32-33
St. 3—Matt. 27:57-66; John 19:38-42
St. 4—John 20:1-18; Acts 2:24; Eph. 1:19-20
St. 5—Matt. 16:27; Luke 21:27; Acts 1:11; 1 Cor. 15:52; 1 Thess. 4:15-17; Titus 2:13; Rev. 1:7

263—ONLY TRUST HIM

Through trust in Jesus and his blood and his word, we will be saved.

John 3:16; 5:24; Acts 10:43; Rom. 3:22-28; 5:1-2
St. 1—Matt. 11:28
St. 2—Isa. 1:18
St. 3—Jer. 17:7; John 14:6

264—ONWARD, CHRISTIAN SOLDIERS

Individuals and church follow Christ as soldiers engaged in spiritual warfare

Matt. 16:18; 1 Cor. 16:13; Eph. 6:10-20; Phil. 1:29-30; 1 Tim. 6:12; 2 Tim. 2:3-4; 4:7-8
St. 1—Deut. 31:8
St. 2—1 Cor. 15:54-58
St. 3—Ps. 133:1; Eph. 4:3-6
St. 4—2 Tim. 4:7-8

265—OPEN MY EYES

Desire to see God's truth, hear his voice, and share his truth

Ps. 40:8; Ezek. 36:27; Matt. 13:16; Mark 8:18; Col. 1:9

St. 1—Ps. 119:18; John 8:32
St. 2—Prov. 15:31; Matt. 11:15
St. 3—Exod. 4:12; Rom. 5:5; Eph. 4:15

OUT IN THE HIGHWAYS—See **MAKE ME A BLESSING**

266—OUT OF MY BONDAGE, SORROW AND NIGHT
Consideration of the varied needs of those who come to Christ

Ps. 86:1-7; Isa. 25:4; 61:1; Matt. 11:28; John 6:37; Acts 16:30-31; Rom. 8:1-2; 2 Thess. 2:14; 1 Tim. 1:15; Rev. 3:20; 22:17

267—OPEN NOW THY GATES OF BEAUTY
Worship in God's presence

Gen. 28:16-17; Ps. 50:2; 118:19-21; 1 John 3:24

268—PEACE, PERFECT PEACE
Jesus gives perfect peace to us in all the challenges to our faith.

Ps. 29:11; Isa. 25:8; 26:3; John 14:27; 16:33; Rom. 15:13; Phil. 4:7

PRAISE GOD FROM WHOM ALL BLESSINGS FLOW—See **DOXOLOGY**

269—PRAISE HIM! PRAISE HIM!
Praise and adoration of Christ as Redeemer, Lord, and King

Ps. 71:23; Heb. 1:3-8; 13:8; Rev. 1:5-6; 5:11-14
St. 1—Ps. 66:1-2; 148:2; Isa. 40:11; 44:22-23
St. 2—Isa. 53; Hab. 3:18; Col. 1:14; Heb. 2:7-10; 1 Pet. 2:4; 1 John
     4:9-10
St. 3—Ps. 148:2; Matt. 25:31; Heb. 8:1; Rev. 1:8; 11:15-17

270—PRAISE, MY SOUL, THE KING OF HEAVEN
Worship; praise and adoration to the eternal, omnipotent God for his majesty, power, and his mercy

Ps. 47:6-7; Ps. 103—paraphrase
1 Chron. 29:10-13; Jer. 33:11; 1 Tim. 1:17
St. 1—Ps. 103:1-4; 145:13; Lam. 5:19
St. 2—Ps. 103:5-12
St. 3—Ps. 103:13-18
St. 4—Ps. 103:19-22; 148:2

271—PRAISE THE LORD! YE HEAVENS ADORE HIM

Worship; praise and adoration to the all-powerful God of creation and salvation

Neh. 9:6; Ps. 148—paraphrase
1 Chron. 16:31; Ps. 21:13; 145:10-12, 21; Amos 4:13; Rev. 4:11

272—PRAISE TO GOD, IMMORTAL PRAISE

Praise; thankfulness expressed for God's loving care and for all the blessings we have from him

1 Chron. 16:34; Ps. 7:17; 13:5-6; 67; 107:1; 147:1, 7; Jonah 2:9; 1 Tim. 4:4-5; Heb. 13:15

PRAISE TO THE LIVING GOD—See THE GOD OF ABRAHAM PRAISE

273—PRAISE TO THE LORD, THE ALMIGHTY

Worship; praise to God, our Creator, for his care and for his guidance

Ps. 103:1-4, 20; Rev. 19:6b-7a
Job 22:26; Ps. 97:1; 100; 104; 150; Col. 1:15-20
St. 1—Ps. 103:1-4
St. 2—Ps. 37:4-5; 93
St. 3—Ps. 103:2
St. 4—Ps. 103:1; 106:48

274—PRAYER IS THE SOUL'S SINCERE DESIRE

Prayer as the expression of the soul's feelings; prayer as the Christian's breath

Ps. 6:9; 65:2; 130:2; Matt. 6:5-13; Rom. 8:26; 1 Cor. 14:15; 1 John 5:14-15
Last st.—John 14:6

275—REDEEMED, HOW I LOVE TO PROCLAIM IT

Expression of the joy of one redeemed by the blood of Christ

Ps. 107:2; Rom. 3:24-26; Eph. 1:7; Col. 1:12-14; 1 Pet. 1:18-19; 1 John 3:1; Rev. 5:9

276—REJOICE, THE LORD IS KING

Christ as King; praise and adoration; joy; resurrection

Phil. 4:4
Ps. 145:1-2, 13; Zech. 14:9; Matt. 28:18; Luke 1:32-33, 47; John 16:33; Rom. 6:9-10; 9:5; 14:8-9; Phil. 2:9-11; Col. 3:1; 1 Tim. 1:17; Heb. 1:3; 7:26; Rev. 1:18; 11:15

277—REJOICE, YE PURE IN HEART
Worship; grateful praise and adoration; processional

Ps. 20:4-5; 24; 32:11; 33:1; 60:4; 147:1, 7; 148:12-13; Phil. 4:4; Col. 3:16; 1 Tim. 1:15-19; 6:12

278—RESCUE THE PERISHING
Challenge to bring the gospel to every person in need; worldwide missions and ministry

Isa. 6:8; 61:1; Mark 16:15-16; Luke 14:23; 19:10; Acts 26:18; 2 Pet. 3:9
St. 2—John 3:36; Acts 10:43; Rom. 2:4; 2 Pet. 3:9
St. 3—Rom. 16:20; 1 Cor. 10:13
St. 4—Acts 1:8; 1 Cor. 15:10

279—REVIVE US AGAIN
Expression of praise and prayer for spiritual renewal

Ps. 85:6; Matt. 3:11; 1 Cor. 1:31; 2:2; 15:57; 2 Cor. 4:6, 16; 9:15; Titus 3:5-6; Heb. 10:12; Rev. 5:12-13

280—RIDE ON! RIDE ON IN MAJESTY
Palm Sunday; Christ as King; suffering and death of Christ

Zech. 9:9; Matt. 21:1-11; John 12:12-15; Heb. 1:3; Rev. 1:5-6

281—RISE UP, O MEN OF GOD
Call to men to give their all to Christ and to his church

Luke 17:10; John 12:26; 21:15-17; Eph. 6:7; 1 Pet. 2:17
St. 1—Deut. 11:13; Matt. 22:37
St. 2—Heb. 10:37
St. 3—Acts 20:28
St. 4—Matt. 12:50; Gal. 6:14

282—ROCK OF AGES
Atonement; Christ as the rock of our salvation; grace; security; cross and blood of Christ

Exod. 17:1-6; 33:17-23; Ps. 78:35; John 19:34; Acts 4:12; Rom. 5:6-11;
1 Cor. 3:11; 10:4; Eph. 2:8, 13; Col. 1:20-23; Heb. 1:3; Rev. 3:20-21;
7:15-17

283—SAFELY THROUGH ANOTHER WEEK
Worship on the Lord's Day

Gen. 2:2-3; Exod. 20:8-11; 31:16-17; Lev. 23:3; Isa. 66:23; Mark 2:27-
28; Heb. 10:1-25

284—SAVIOR, AGAIN TO THY DEAR NAME
Evening; benediction; peace from an ever-present God

Ps. 4:8; Isa. 26:3, 12-13; 57:2; Luke 1:79; John 14:27; Rom. 15:33;
Eph. 2:14-18; 6:23-24; 2 Thess. 3:16; Heb. 13:20-21

285—SAVIOR, BREATHE AN EVENING BLESSING
Evening; calmness that the presence of Christ as Savior brings

Ps. 63:6-8; 73:24; 91:5-6; 141:2; Rom. 14:7-9
St. 1—Exod. 34:9; Ps. 141:2
St. 2—Ps. 91:5-6, 10-11
St. 3—Ps. 139:11-12
St. 4—1 Cor. 15:51-53

286—SAVIOR, LIKE A SHEPHERD LEAD US
Jesus' care and guidance as shepherd over sheep

Isa. 40:11; Ezek. 34:23; John 10:14-16, 27
St. 1—Ps. 23:1-2; Ezek. 34:14-15; John 10:14-15; 1 Cor. 7:23
St. 2—Ps. 23:3; Mic. 7:7; Matt. 18:12; 2 Thess. 3:3; 1 Pet. 2:25
St. 3—Ps. 103:10-12; Prov. 8:17; John 6:37; Titus 3:5; Heb. 4:16
St. 4—Prov. 8:17; Eph. 2:4; Heb. 13:20-21

287—SAVIOR, TEACH ME DAY BY DAY
We learn of Christ's love and we love and serve him because he first
loved us.

John 13:34; 21:15-17; Eph. 3:17-19; 5:2; 1 Thess. 4:9; 1 John 3:16; 4:19

288—SAVIOR, THY DYING LOVE
Expresses the responses a Christian makes to the love shown by
Christ on the cross

Matt. 23:23; Luke 10:27; Rom. 12:1; Eph. 5:2; 1 Pet. 4:10; 1 John 3:16; 4:19
St. 4—Matt. 25:21

289—SHEPHERD OF TENDER [EAGER] YOUTH
Youth; guidance sought; Christ as Shepherd

Ps. 23; Ezek. 34:12-16; Rom. 14:9; 1 Pet. 2:24-25; Rev. 7:17
St. 2—Eph. 2:4-5
St. 3—Heb. 8:1
St. 4—Ps. 23:3

290—SILENT NIGHT! HOLY NIGHT
Birth of Jesus; Nativity setting

Matt. 2:9-10; Luke 1:77-79; 2:7-20

SIMPLY TRUSTING EVERY DAY—See TRUSTING JESUS

291—SINCE I HAVE BEEN REDEEMED
Testimony; joy of one who has been redeemed

Ps. 107:2; Rom. 15:9; Eph. 1:3, 7; Col. 1:12-14; Titus 2:14
St. 2—Ps. 107:9; Phil. 2:13
St. 3—Ps. 34:4
St. 4—John 14:2; 2 Cor. 5:1

292—SING PRAISE TO GOD WHO REIGNS ABOVE
All praise and glory to an omnipotent God of creation, but also a God who is always close to us

1 Chron. 16:25-36; Ps. 47:6-7; 118:28-29; 146; Isa. 12:2-5; Heb. 13:15; 1 Pet. 2:9
St. 2—Ps. 121:4
St. 3—Ps. 139:7

SING THE WONDROUS LOVE OF JESUS—See WHEN WE ALL GET TO HEAVEN

SING THEM OVER AGAIN TO ME—See WONDERFUL WORDS OF LIFE

SINNERS JESUS WILL RECEIVE—See **CHRIST RECEIVETH SINFUL MEN**

293—SOFTLY AND TENDERLY
Jesus calls, pleads, and waits for us as sinners and he promises mercy and pardon.

Prov. 1:24; Isa. 55:7; Matt. 11:28; 25:34; John 10:3; 11:28; 1 Thess. 5:24; Rev. 3:20; 22:17

294—SOFTLY NOW THE LIGHT OF DAY
Evening; communion with God

Exod. 34:9; Ps. 4:8; 42:8; 63:6-8; 141:2; Isa. 26:9; 58:8; John 12:35-36

295—SOLDIERS OF CHRIST, ARISE
Equipped with the proper spiritual armor, we press on to victory in the Christian life and spiritual warfare.

Rom. 8:37; 1 Cor. 15:57-58; 2 Cor. 12:9; Eph. 6:10-20; Phil. 1:27-30; 1 Tim. 6:12; 2 Tim. 2:3-4; 4:7-8

SOMETHING FOR THEE—See **SAVIOR, THY DYING LOVE**

296—SOMETIMES A LIGHT SURPRISES
Expression of joy, peace, hope, and confidence in faith

Matt. 6:25-34; 2 Cor. 4:6; Heb. 3:6
St. 1—2 Sam. 23:4; Isa. 60:1; Mal. 4:2
St. 2—Ps. 35:9; Isa. 12:2; Matt. 6:34
St. 3—Luke 12:22-28
St. 4—Hab. 3:17-18

297—SPIRIT DIVINE, ATTEND OUR PRAYER
Holy Spirit; prayer; aspiration; prayer for presence of the Holy Spirit

Acts 9:31
Ezek. 36:27; Matt. 3:11; John 14:16-17; Acts 1:8; 2:1-4; 4:31; Rom. 8:9; Gal. 5:25

298—SPIRIT OF GOD, DESCEND UPON MY HEART
Prayer that the Spirit of God would dwell in us and take complete control; Holy Spirit; God is adequate for all needs; Christian experience

Job 32:8; 33:4; Ps. 51:10-12; John 15:26; Rom. 5:5; 8:1-4; Gal. 5:25;
2 Tim. 1:7
St. 1—Eph. 3:16
St. 3—Luke 10:27

299—STAND UP AND BLESS THE LORD
Worship; eternal praise to an almighty God; devotion; courage

1 Chron. 23:30; Neh. 9:5; Ps. 63:4; 103; 134
St. 1—Ps. 51:15; 103:1; 1 Pet. 2:9
St. 2—Ps. 2:11; 22:23; Heb. 12:28
St. 3—Ps. 17:1; Rom. 8:26
St. 4—Ps. 103:3-4; John 13:34-35; 1 John 4:7-21
St. 5—1 Chron. 16:36; Ps. 145:1-2

300—STAND UP, STAND UP FOR JESUS
In strength of Christ, we engage in spiritual warfare, pressing on to
victory and crown.

Rom. 8:37; 1 Cor. 15:57-58; 16:13; Eph. 6:10-20; Phil. 1:27-30; 1 Tim.
6:12; 2 Tim. 2:3-4; 4:7-8; Heb. 10:23

301—STANDING ON THE PROMISES
Expression of dependence on the promises of God

Acts 2:38-39; Rom. 4:20; 2 Cor. 1:20-22; Gal. 3:14-22, 29; Heb. 9:15;
10:23; James 1:12; 2 Pet. 1:4; 1 John 2:25

302—STILL, STILL WITH THEE
Morning; communion with God; worship

Ps. 139:17-18
1 Chron. 23:30; Job 19:25-27; Ps. 3:5; 5:3; 30:5; 59:16; 73:24; Col. 3:4;
1 John 4:13

303—STRONG SON OF GOD
Confession of faith and consecration to a great Savior

Matt. 12:6; Luke 1:37; Gal. 4:4; Eph. 3:19; Phil. 2:5-11
St. 1—John 20:29
Last st.—Prov. 2:3-5

304—SUN OF MY SOUL, THOU SAVIOR DEAR
God as our light; prayer for God's presence and blessing; worship; praise; love of Christ

Luke 1:77-79; 24:29
Ps. 4:6-8; 84:11; 139:1-12; 2 Cor. 4:4; 1 Pet. 2:9

305—SUNSHINE IN MY SOUL
In the presence of Jesus there is light like sunshine and joy in our lives.

John 1:4; 8:12; 15:11; 2 Cor. 4:6

306—SURELY GOODNESS AND MERCY
Jesus as Guardian and Shepherd of our lives; anticipation of heaven

Ps. 23
Exod. 15:13; Ps. 16:11; 48:14; 106:1
St. 1—Rom. 2:4; 1 Pet. 2:25
St. 2—Ps. 23:3; 27:1; 51:15
St. 3—Ps. 23:4; John 14:2
Refrain—Ps. 23:6; Luke 14:15; Rev. 19:9

307—SWEET HOUR OF PRAYER
We take all our cares and needs to God in prayer.

Ps. 5:3; 6:9; 55:22; 65:2; Matt. 6:5-13; Phil. 4:6; 1 Pet. 5:7
St. 3—Deut. 3:27

308—TAKE MY LIFE AND LET IT BE
Personal expression of complete consecration to God

1 Chron. 29:5; Matt. 22:37; Rom. 6:13; 12:1; 1 Cor. 6:19-20; 2 Tim. 2:20-21

309—TAKE THE NAME OF JESUS WITH YOU
The name of Jesus

Matt. 12:21; John 14:13; 20:31; Acts 4:12; Phil. 2:9-10; Col. 3:17; Heb. 13:15

310—TAKE TIME TO BE HOLY
Holiness and spiritual maturity require a close relationship with Jesus as Lord and Master of our lives.

Lev. 20:7-8; Eph. 4:24; Heb. 12:14

St. 1—Matt. 4:4; John 15:4-5; Rom. 15:1
St. 2—Matt. 6:6; John 13:15
St. 3—Ps. 48:14; 118:8; Prov. 3:5
St. 4—Ps. 143:10; John 16:13; 1 Thess. 3:12-13

TAKE UP THY CROSS AND FOLLOW ME—See WHEREVER HE LEADS I'LL GO

311—"TAKE UP THY CROSS," THE SAVIOR SAID
We take up our crosses and follow Christ; Christ gives strength; we follow Christ's example; our service leads to victory.

Matt. 16:24-27; Luke 9:57-62; John 12:26; 2 Cor. 12:9-10; 1 Pet. 2:21

312—TELL ME THE STORY OF JESUS
Life of Jesus recalled: birth, temptation, humiliation, crucifixion, and resurrection

Matt. 20:28; Mark 8:31; Acts 10:38-41
St. 1—Luke 2:13-14
St. 2—Isa. 53:3-4; Matt. 4:23; Luke 4:1-14
St. 3—Mark 15:46; 16:6; John 19:17-18; 1 Cor. 15:3-4; 1 Tim. 2:6

313—TEN THOUSAND TIMES TEN THOUSAND
Immortal life; anticipation and desire for heaven expressed
Rev. 21-22
Isa. 35:10; 1 Cor. 15:54-57; 2 Cor. 5:8; Heb. 12:22; Jude 14; Rev. 5:11-12; 19:6

314—THE CHURCH'S ONE FOUNDATION
Christ created the church and is its foundation; supremacy of the church

Matt. 16:15-18; Acts 2:42, 47; 1 Cor. 3:11; Eph. 1:22-23; 2:19-22; Col. 1:18; Heb. 3:1-6
St. 1—Eph. 5:23, 25-27
St. 2—1 Cor. 10:17; Eph. 4:4-6
Last st.—Rev. 2:7

315—THE DAY OF RESURRECTION
Resurrection of Christ; joy; praise

Matt. 12:8; 28:1-9; Acts 2:24-28; 1 Cor. 15:57; Rev. 22:3

St. 1—Mark 16:9*a*
St. 2—Isa. 9:2; 2 Cor. 4:6
St. 3—Ps. 148:5

316—THE DAY THOU GAVEST
Evening; praise and prayer continues day and night through the church eternally.

Ps. 113:2-3
Ps. 42:8; 55:17; 92:2; Isa. 26:9; Matt. 16:18; Eph. 3:21
Last st.—Ps. 145:13; Isa. 45:22-23; Lam. 5:19; Luke 1:33

317—THE FIRST NOEL THE ANGELS DID SAY
Birth of Christ; shepherds, wise men, star; praise for God's gift

St. 1—Luke 2:8-20
St. 2—Matt. 2:2, 7, 9, 10
St. 3—Matt. 2:1-12
St. 4—Luke 1:68-79; Gal. 4:4-5; Eph. 1:3-12
Refrain—Luke 1:33

318—THE GOD OF ABRAHAM PRAISE
Praise to an almighty, eternal God

Exod. 3:14; Ps. 22:23; 106:48; Isa. 6:3; Lam. 5:19; John 8:58; Heb. 13:8; Rev. 1:8; 11:17

319—THE GREAT PHYSICIAN
Name of Jesus; compassion and care of Christ; praise; Savior

Matt. 1:21; 9:1-13; 28:20; Acts 10:43; Heb. 1:3; 1 John 2:12
St. 1—Matt. 4:23; 8:8; Luke 7:20-22; Acts 10:38; 2 Cor. 1:5
St. 2—Mark 2:5; Luke 23:34; John 3:3, 16; 2 Cor. 5:8; Eph. 1:7; Heb. 13:14
St. 3, 4, and refrain—Matt. 12:21; John 1:29; Phil. 2:9-11; 1 Pet. 1:7; 1 John 1:7

320—THE HEAD THAT ONCE WAS CROWNED
Exaltation of Christ; eternal life; cross; Christ as King; joy

Phil. 2:5-11; Heb. 2:9-10
John 12:32; 16:19-24; Acts 2:36; 5:30-31; 1 Cor. 15:54; Eph. 2:4-6; Heb. 12:2-4

St. 1—John 19:1-5; Heb. 2:9
St. 2—John 15:11; Rom. 5:11; Phil. 3:8; 1 Thess. 2:19-20; 1 Pet. 1:8
St. 3 & 4—Gal. 6:14; Eph. 2:16; Col. 1:20

321—THE HEAVENS DECLARE THY GLORY
God's Word is greater than all the creations of God found in nature;
Word as guide to heaven

Ps. 19; 119:89, 161; 138:2; 2 Tim. 3:16-17; 1 Pet. 1:24-25
St. 4—John 15:3

322—THE KING OF LOVE MY SHEPHERD IS
Jesus' care for us compared to that of a shepherd for his sheep

Ps. 23—paraphrase
Ps. 95:7; John 10:14-15, 27
St. 1—Ps. 23:1
St. 2—Ps. 23:2; John 10:9; Rev. 22:17
St. 3—Ps. 23:3; Isa. 53:6; Luke 15:3-7; 1 Pet. 2:25
St. 4—Ps. 23:4; Heb. 2:14-15
St. 5—Ps. 23:6; 79:13; 84:4

323—THE LIGHT OF THE WORLD IS JESUS
Christ as the light of life; Savior; hope

John 1:4-9; 8:12
Isa. 9:2; 60:1-3; Mic. 7:8; Luke 1:77-79; 2:29-32; John 3:19-21; 12:35-
36, 46; Eph. 5:8-14; 1 John 1:7; 2:8; Rev. 21:23-24

324—THE LILY OF THE VALLEY
Christ as friend and present in all the needs of life; praise; name of
Christ

Song of Sol. 2:1; 5:10; Rev. 22:16
Job 19:25-27; Ps. 55:22; 94:19; 138:7; Matt. 11:28-30; 28:20; John
7:38; 14:1-4; Rom. 8:35-39; 1 Cor. 15:57; 2 Cor. 1:3-7; 12:9; Phil. 4:13;
Col. 1:11; 1 Thess. 4:17; Heb. 2:18; 13:5-6; 1 Pet. 5:7; 1 John 1:7-9;
Rev. 2:17; 22:1

325—THE LORD IS MY SHEPHERD or THE LORD'S MY SHEPHERD or THE LORD MY SHEPHERD IS

Ps. 23—paraphrase
Ps. 78:52; Isa. 40:11; John 10:1-6; Heb. 13:20-21; 1 Pet. 5:7

326—THE LORD WILL COME
Second Coming of Christ; kingdom; judgment

Isa. 9:7; Matt. 25:31-33; Luke 21:22; John 5:22, 27; Acts 17:31;
Rom. 2:16; 2 Thess. 1:7-10; 2 Pet. 3:3-14; Rev. 11:15-18
St. 1—Ps. 85:11-13; Heb. 10:37; James 5:7-9
St. 2—Ps. 96:13; 98:8-9
St. 3—Ps. 82:8; Rom. 2:5; Jude 15
St. 4—Ps. 86:10; Zech. 14:9

327—THE MORNING LIGHT IS BREAKING
An optimistic expression concerning a coming new day in world
evangelism

Ps. 85:6; Matt. 4:16; Acts 17:30; 1 Cor. 15:34; Eph. 5:14

328—THE OLD RUGGED CROSS
Atonement; cross, suffering, and death of Christ; salvation

John 14:2-3; 19:17; Rom. 5:6-11; 1 Cor. 1:17-18; Gal. 6:14; Eph. 2:16;
Phil. 2:8; Col. 1:20-23; 2:13-15; Heb. 1:3; 12:2; 1 Pet. 2:24; 4:13; Rev.
1:5-6; 5:9-10

329—THE SOLID ROCK
Describes our hope of salvation as Jesus' blood, righteousness,
unchanging grace, oath, and covenant; hope as basis of faith

John 14:6; Acts 4:12; Rom. 5:1-5; 1 Cor. 3:11; 1 Tim. 2:5; Heb. 6:17-
19; 1 Pet. 1:3; 3:15

330—THE SON OF GOD GOES FORTH TO WAR
We follow Christ as leading us in spiritual warfare.

1 Cor. 16:13; Eph. 6:10-20; Phil. 1:27-30; 1 Tim. 6:12; 2 Tim. 2:3-4;
4:7-8; Heb. 2:10; 10:23; 1 Pet. 5:8-9; Jude 3; Rev. 17:14
St. 1—Luke 9:23; Mark 10:38
St. 2—Acts 7:54-60
Last st.—Rev. 7:9-17

331—THE SPACIOUS FIRMAMENT
Praise; acknowledgment of the majesty and power of God and his
creation; worship

Gen. 1:1-19; Ps. 19:1-6; Isa. 40:26; 48:13; Jer. 10:12-13; (*next page*)

Acts 17:24; Rom. 1:20; Heb. 11:3

332—THE STRIFE IS O'ER
Joy; praise to God for Jesus' resurrection and victory over death

Ps. 96:1-2; Isa. 25:7-9; 53:5; Mark 10:34; Luke 24:6; Rom. 1:4; 6:9-10; 1 Cor. 15:54-57; 1 Pet. 2:24; Rev. 19:1-2

THE WHOLE WORLD WAS LOST—See THE LIGHT OF THE WORLD IS JESUS

333—THERE IS A FOUNTAIN
Blood of Christ; atonement; cross; salvation

Zech. 13:1; John 19:34
Ps. 36:9; Matt. 26:28; Luke 22:20; Eph. 1:7; 2:13; Heb. 9:14; 10:19; 13:10-12; 1 Pet. 1:19; 1 John 1:7; Rev. 1:5-6; 5:9

334—THERE IS A GREEN HILL FAR AWAY
Suffering and death of Christ; cross of Christ; atonement; love of Christ; salvation; our love to God

Heb. 13:12
John 19:17-18; Acts 4:12; Rom. 5:6-11; Eph. 1:7-8; 2:13-18; 5:2; Col. 1:13-14, 20-23; 1 Thess. 5:9-10; 1 Tim. 2:5-6; Titus 2:14; Heb. 13:10-14; 1 Pet. 2:24; 3:18; 1 John 3:5

THERE IS A NAME I LOVE TO HEAR—See O HOW I LOVE JESUS

335—THERE IS POWER IN THE BLOOD
The blood of Christ has power to cleanse and pardon from sin.

Isa. 1:18; Zech. 13:1; Rom. 3:24-25; Eph. 1:7-8; 2:13; Heb. 9:14; 1 Pet. 1:18-19

336—THERE'S A SONG IN THE AIR
Birth of Jesus; all earth praises him for eternity; the birth of a King

Matt. 2:10; Luke 1:33, 68-69; 2:9-20, 29-32

337—THERE'S A WIDENESS IN GOD'S MERCY
God's boundless love and mercy to mankind

Ps. 36:5; 86:5, 15; 98:9; 103:8-13; Lam. 3:22-23; John 3:16; Rom. 8:35-

39; 2 Cor. 12:9; Eph. 1:6-8; 2:4; 1 John 1:7; 4:8-19

THERE'S NOT A FRIEND LIKE THE LOWLY JESUS—See **NO, NOT ONE**

THERE'S WITHIN MY HEART A MELODY—See **HE KEEPS ME SINGING**

338—THIS IS MY FATHER'S WORLD
God's majesty, power, love, care, and guidance as revealed in nature and in Jesus Christ

Ps. 8; 19:1; 24:1; 145:10-13; Matt. 12:20-21; John 16:33; Rom. 16:20; 1 Cor. 15:25-26; Heb. 2:14-15; 2 Pet. 3:13; Rev. 12:10

339—THIS IS THE DAY THE LORD HATH MADE
Lord's Day; worship; praise; day of resurrection

Ps. 118:24; Matt. 12:8; John 20:1-20
St. 1—Gen. 1:3-5; Exod. 20:8-11; Lev. 23:1-3
St. 2—Matt. 28:6-7; Eph. 2:4-6; Rev. 1:18
St. 3 & 4—Zech. 9:9; Matt. 9:27; 21:5, 9; Mark 11:9;
         2 Tim. 2:8; Rev. 17:14

340—THOU ART THE WAY: TO THEE ALONE
Christ as the only way to God; Christ as truth; Christ as life

John 14:6
John 5:24; 10:9-10
St. 1—Eph. 2:18; 1 Tim. 2:5
St. 2—John 8:32; 16:13; 17:19
St. 3—John 11:25; 2 Tim. 1:10; 1 John 5:12

341—THOU DIDST LEAVE THY THRONE
Christ: birth, life, and ministry; humility of Jesus' coming; invitation to acceptance of Christ

Luke 2:7
Ps. 24:7; 27:8; 51:10; Zech. 10:7; Matt. 8:20; 2 Cor. 8:9; Phil. 2:5-11; 1 Thess. 3:13; Heb. 1:2-8; 4:7; 1 Pet. 3:22

342—THOU WHOSE ALMIGHTY WORD
Missions; desire that there would be "light" throughout the world

Gen. 1:3; Isa. 9:2; 60:1-3; John 8:12; Acts 26:18; 2 Cor. 4:6; 1 John 1:5
St. 1—Gen. 1:2-3
St. 2—Mal. 4:2; Matt. 15:30
St. 3—Acts 1:8

343—'TIS MIDNIGHT AND ON OLIVE'S BROW
Christ in Gethsemane; prayer; suffering and death

Matt. 26:30, 36-45; Mark 14:26, 32-41; Luke 22:29-44; John 18:1

344—'TIS SO SWEET TO TRUST IN JESUS
Expression of complete trust in Jesus for salvation and full life

Ps. 37:5; John 5:24; 6:68; 20:29, 31; Acts 10:43; Rom. 1:16-17; 5:1-2;
Eph. 1:12-13
St. 4—Matt. 28:20

345—TO GOD BE THE GLORY
Praise and adoration to God for all that he has done for us through
Christ; gospel; joy

Gal. 1:5; Eph. 5:20; 1 Tim. 1:15-17
Ps. 29:2; 72:18-19; 138:5; John 1:14; 3:16-17; 1 Cor. 6:20; 10:31; Col.
3:17; 1 Pet. 1:2-3; 1 John 4:14; Rev. 1:5

TRUST AND OBEY—See WHEN WE WALK WITH THE LORD

346—TRUSTING JESUS
Expression of simple, uncomplicated trust

Ps. 37:3-5; 56:3-4; Prov. 3:5; 2 Cor. 3:4-5; Eph. 6:16; 2 Tim. 1:12-13;
1 John 5:4-5

347—WALK IN THE LIGHT
God is the light of our lives and if we walk in that light, we experience
his loving presence and fellowship.

Ps. 36:9; Isa. 9:2; John 8:12; Eph. 5:8; Col. 2:6; 1 John 1:5-7

348—WATCHMAN, TELL US OF THE NIGHT
Expression of anticipation of a new day in Christ

Isa. 21:11-12
Isa. 60:1-3; Rom. 13:12

349—WE GATHER TOGETHER
Hymn of petition and thanks; God as Defender and Guide; Christian warfare

Deut. 31:8; Ps. 5:11; 32:8; Acts 14:22; Rom. 8:31
St. 1—Ps. 94:12; 119:134; Heb. 12:5-7
St. 2—Ps. 145:13
St. 3—John 16:33

350—WE GIVE THEE BUT THINE OWN
Obligation to Christian stewardship and to the needs that are met thereby

Gen. 28:22; Lev. 27:30-33; 1 Chron. 29:14; Hag. 2:8; Mal. 3:8-10; 1 Cor. 16:2; 2 Cor. 9:6-7
St. 4—Matt. 6:1-4

351—WE HAVE HEARD THE JOYFUL SOUND
We are commanded to spread the gospel to every land by song and spoken word.

Ps. 67:2; 71:15; 96:1-3; Isa. 52:7; Mark 16:15; Luke 24:47; Acts 1:8; 4:12; Rom. 1:16

WE MAY NOT CLIMB THE HEAVENLY STEEPS—See IMMORTAL LOVE, FOREVER FULL

352—WE PLOW THE FIELDS
All good gifts come from God; thanks for God's providential care

Gen. 1:11-18; 2:4-5; Ps. 65:9-11; 103:2; Isa. 55:10; Acts 14:17; Phil. 4:19; Heb. 11:3; 13:15; James 1:17

WE PRAISE THEE, O GOD, FOR THE SON—See REVIVE US AGAIN

353—WE PRAISE THEE, O GOD, OUR REDEEMER
Praise and adoration for God's loving care and guidance and for the redemption he provides

Luke 1:68
Gen. 28:15-16; Ps. 61:8; 71:6-8; 111:1; 118:21; Isa. 60:16; Rev. 19:1
St. 1—Ps. 9:1-2; 78:35; Isa. 47:4
St. 2—Ps. 16:8; Isa. 40:28-31 (*see next page*)

St. 3—Ps. 67:5; 96:1-2; 145:1-2

354—WE THREE KINGS
Visit of wise men to baby Jesus; Christmas
Matt. 2:1-11

355—WE WOULD SEE JESUS, LO! HIS STAR
Christ: birth, life, and ministry; discipleship
John 12:21
Matt. 2:2; 16:28; 23:39
St. 1—Matt. 2:1-2, 9-11; Luke 2:7, 13-14
St. 2—Luke 1:77-79; 2:52; John 1:4-9; 14:4-6
St. 3—Matt. 5:1-2; Ps. 128:1
St. 4—Isa. 6:8; Matt. 10:38; 16:24-26; John 10:4; 12:26; Rom. 12:1, 11

356—WE'RE MARCHING TO ZION
Songs of praise of saints marching to Zion, the beautiful city of God;
joy
Ps. 50:2; 144:15; 149:1-2; Isa. 35:10; Eph. 5:19; Heb. 13:15; Rev. 21:2

357—WE'VE A STORY TO TELL TO THE NATIONS
Missions; reminder of the promise that Christ's kingdom will come
only when every "tribe and tongue" has heard the gospel
Ps. 67:2; 96:2-3; Isa. 9:2; 52:7; Matt. 24:14; Mark 16:15; Luke 24:47;
John 12:46; Acts 1:8; 26:17-18; Rom. 1:16
St. 3—John 3:16; 1 John 4:10
St. 4—Isa. 53:3; John 1:29

358—WELCOME, HAPPY MORNING
Joy; praise; resurrection of Christ
Matt. 12:8; 28:1-9; Mark 16:9a; 1 Cor. 15:20; Rev. 20:14; 21:22-25

359—WERE YOU THERE
Remembrance of the crucifixion of Jesus, his burial, and his
resurrection
Matt. 27:27-60; Mark 15:25; John 19:16-18; Phil. 2:8; Col. 2:14

WHAT A FELLOWSHIP—See **LEANING ON THE EVERLASTING ARMS**

360—WHAT A FRIEND WE HAVE IN JESUS
Need of taking all needs in life to the Lord in prayer; prayer; Jesus as Friend

Ps. 6:9; 55:22; 57:1; Mark 11:24; John 15:13-16; Rom. 12:12; Phil. 4:6; 1 Thess. 5:17; 1 Pet. 5:7; 1 John 5:14-15

361—WHAT A WONDERFUL SAVIOR
Christ as Savior; atonement; praise; salvation; blood of Christ

Isa. 53:4-12; Rom. 5:6-11; Eph. 2:4-7; Titus 2:14; Heb. 13:20-21; 1 Pet. 1:18-19; 1 John 4:9-10; Rev. 1:5-6
St. 1—1 Cor. 6:20
St. 2—Eph. 2:13
St. 3—Rom. 3:21-26
St. 4—Isa. 40:29; Rom. 8:37-39; 1 Cor. 15:57

362—WHAT CHILD IS THIS?
Birth of Jesus

Matt. 2:1-12; Luke 2:6-20

363—WHAT IF IT WERE TODAY?
Return of Christ; reign of Christ as King; praise

Matt. 25:13; Mark 13:32-37; Luke 12:35-40; Luke 21:25-36; Acts 1:9-11; Heb. 9:28; 2 Pet. 3:3-14
St. 1—Matt. 25:1-13; Mark 13:26-27; John 14:3; 2 Pet. 1:16
St. 2—Isa. 25:7-9; Rom. 16:20; 1 Thess. 4:16; Titus 2:13; Rev. 21:4
St. 3—Luke 18:8; Rom. 13:11-12; 2 Pet. 3:14; 1 John 2:28
Refrain—John 16:20-22; 1 Thess. 2:19-20; 1 Tim. 6:15

364—WHAT WONDROUS LOVE IS THIS
We sing of God and his great love expressed to us in Jesus Christ.

John 15:13; Rom. 5:8; Gal. 3:13; Eph. 3:17-19; Phil. 2:6-11; 1 John 3:1, 16; 4:19; Rev. 5:12-13; 7:9-10

WHEN ALL MY LABORS AND TRIALS—See **O THAT WILL BE GLORY**

365—WHEN ALL THY MERCIES, O MY GOD
Acknowledges all the wonderful mercies and goodness of God; God gives comfort, health, and reviving.

1 Chron. 16:34; Ps. 23:6; 31:7; 63:3; 86:5, 15; 89:1; Luke 1:50

366—WHEN I SURVEY THE WONDROUS CROSS
Atonement; Christ's suffering and death on the cross; cross as symbol; love of Christ

1 Cor. 2:2; Phil. 3:7-8; Gal. 6:14
Matt. 26:28; Luke 7:47; John 19:17-18, 34; Rom. 5:6-11; 1 Cor. 1:17-18, 31; Eph. 1:6-8; 2:13; Phil. 3:3-11; Col. 1:13-23; Heb. 9:12-26; 1 Pet. 1:21; 2:24; 1 John 2:15-16

WHEN PEACE LIKE A RIVER—See IT IS WELL WITH MY SOUL

WHEN UPON LIFE'S BILLOWS—See COUNT YOUR BLESSINGS

367—WHEN MORNING GILDS THE SKIES
Worship; praise; morning

1 Chron. 23:30; Ps. 30:4-5; Matt. 28:9; John 5:23; 12:13; 1 Thess. 5:16-18; 2 Pet. 1:19; Rev. 5:12
St. 1—Ps. 5:3; 59:16-17
St. 2—Ps. 33:1; 147:1
St. 3—Ps. 4:6; 139:11-12; Isa. 2:5
St. 4—Ps. 148; 150:6

368—WHEN WE ALL GET TO HEAVEN
Expression of anticipation of heaven

Ps. 16:11; Isa. 35:10; John 14:2-3; Acts 20:32; 1 Cor. 15:54-57; 2 Cor. 5:8; 1 John 2:25; Rev. 14:13
St. 3—1 Pet. 4:13
St. 4—Phil. 3:14; Rev. 21:21

369—WHEN WE WALK WITH THE LORD
Expression of trust and its resulting happiness; balance between law (works) and grace (faith)

Exod. 19:5; Ps. 4:5; 37:3-5; 143:8-10; John 8:31; 14:12, 23; 2 Cor. 5:7; James 2:14-26; 1 John 2:6

370—WHERE CROSS THE CROWDED WAYS
Social gospel; service

Zech. 7:9; Matt. 9:36; 10:42; Mark 9:41; Luke 19:41; John 13:34-35; Eph. 6:6; 1 John 3:17

371—WHERE HE LEADS ME
Jesus leads and we follow, taking up our crosses; he will go with us as we follow him.

Matt. 8:19; 20:22; Luke 9:23; John 12:26; 2 Cor. 1:5

372—WHEREVER HE LEADS I'LL GO
We take up our crosses and follow Jesus, giving him our all; we seek and live in his will.

Mark 10:21, 43-45; Luke 9:23; John 12:26; Eph. 5:17; 1 Pet. 2:21
St. 4—Matt. 22:37

373—WHILE SHEPHERDS WATCHED THEIR FLOCKS
Birth of Christ; shepherds' visit by angels; praise

Luke 2:8-14
St. 1—Luke 2:8-9
St. 2—Luke 2:10
St. 3—Luke 1:69; 2:11-12; Rom. 1:3
St. 4—Luke 2:12
St. 5—Luke 2:13-14

374—WHITER THAN SNOW
Blood of Christ cleanses and gives new heart

Ps. 51:2, 7; Isa. 1:18; Zech. 13:1; Rom. 3:24-25; 12:1-2; 1 Cor. 6:11; Heb. 9:14; 1 John 1:7, 9

375—WHO IS ON THE LORD'S SIDE?
Commitment to follow Christ in spiritual warfare

Exod. 32:26; Josh. 24:15; Rom. 16:20; 2 Cor. 12:9; Eph. 6:10-20; 1 Tim. 6:12; 2 Tim. 2:1-4; Rev. 17:14

376—WHOSOEVER WILL
Universal invitation of the gospel

Rev. 22:17

Luke 11:10; John 3:15-17; Acts 2:21; 10:34, 43; Rom. 10:11-13

377—WONDERFUL WORDS OF LIFE
Jesus has the words of life—wonderful words.

Ps. 119:172; Matt. 4:4; John 5:24; 6:68; 20:31; 1 Thess. 2:13

WONDROUS LOVE—See WHAT WONDROUS LOVE IS THIS

WOULD YOU BE FREE?—See THERE IS POWER IN THE BLOOD

378—YE CHRISTIAN HERALDS
Missions

Ps. 96:2-3; Isa. 6:8; 52:7; Matt. 24:14; Mark 16:15; Acts 1:8; Rom. 10:13-15

379—YE MUST BE BORN AGAIN
Necessity of the new birth for salvation

John 3:3, 7
John 3:1-8; Rom. 6:4; 2 Cor. 5:17; 1 Pet. 1:23; 1 John 5:1

380—YE SERVANTS OF GOD
Christ as King; majesty and power of God; praise

Rev. 7:9-12
Deut. 32:3; Ps. 96:1-10; Phil. 2:9-11; 1 Tim. 6:16; Jude 24-25; Rev. 1:5-6; 5:9-14; 22:3

YEARS I SPENT IN VANITY AND PRIDE—See AT CALVARY

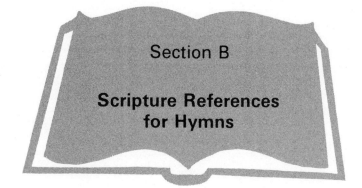

Section B

Scripture References
for Hymns

GENESIS

28:22	# 16		# 115—st.2		# 283
	# 350		# 195		# 339
31:3	# 96—st.3		# 197	**23:16**	# 68
	# 137	**14:27-31**	115—st.2	**24:12**	# 45—st.3
	# 241	**15:1-21**	# 67		# 83
31:13	# 227—st.4	**15:2**	# 102	**25:17-22**	# 66—st.1
32:12	# 185—st.4		# 105	**25:22**	# 66
35:2	# 23—st.4		# 137		# 90
	# 237		# 180	**26:34**	# 66—st.1
35:6	# 227—st.4		# 291		# 90
35:15	# 227—st.4	**15:11**	# 63—st.1	**29:45**	# 96—st.3
41:38	# 298		# 131		# 137
45:11	# 51—st.2		# 132		# 241
47:9	# 127		# 318	**30:6**	# 66—st.1
48:15-16	# 105	**15:13**	# 115		# 90
48:21	# 115		# 125	**31:12-17**	# 236
49:10	# 70—st.3		# 162—st.2		# 339
49:25	# 64		# 198	**32:16**	# 45
	# 349		# 306		# 83
49:25-26	# 69	**15:18**	# 63—st.1	**32:26**	# 261
50:21	# 51—st.2		# 256		# 375
		16:4	# 115—st.1	**32:29**	# 288—st.4
EXODUS		**16:4-10**	# 96—st.3		# 308
		16:4-18	# 115—st.1	**33:14**	# 4
3:2	# 210	**16:7**	# 32		# 25
3:5	# 73	**16:23-30**	# 236		# 57—st.2
	# 100		# 283		# 71
3:12	# 96—st.3		# 339		# 96—st.3
	# 137	**16:35**	# 99—st.2		# 99
	# 241	**17:1-6**	# 96—st.2		# 137
3:14	# 318		# 282		# 143—st.1
	# 364	**18:11**	# 256		# 198
3:15	# 105	**19:5**	# 369		# 226
	# 270	**19:6**	# 310	**33:17-23**	# 282
4:12	# 265—st.3	**19:18**	# 210	**33:20**	# 159
4:31	# 38	**20:3**	# 172—st.2 & 3	**33:22**	# 123
	# 100	**20:4**	# 237	**34:6**	# 33
6:2-3	# 63—st.1	**20:8-11**	# 236		# 101
	# 105		# 283		# 203
6:6	# 51		# 339		# 278—st.2
10:23	# 342	**20:11**	# 138		# 337
12:27	# 38		# 151		# 365
13:21	# 198	**20:12**	# 118	**34:8**	# 38
	# 210		# 243		# 100
	# 378—st.2	**23:12**	# 236	**34:9**	# 283—st.2
13:21-22	# 96—st.3				

EXODUS

	# 285—st.1
34:17	# 237
34:21	# 236
	# 283
	# 339
35:2-3	# 236
	# 283
	# 339

LEVITICUS

7:12-15	# 68
	# 230
	# 352
11:44	# 37
11:45	# 310
16:2	# 66—st.1
	# 90
16:31	# 236
17:11	# 42—st.3
	# 116—st.2
	# 217—st.2
	# 240—st.4
	# 244—st.2
	# 269—st.2
	# 361
19:2	# 37
	# 132
	# 310
19:3	# 236
	# 283
	# 339
19:30	# 100
	# 339
20:7-8	# 310
22:29	# 68
	# 230
	# 352
23:1-3	# 236
	# 283
	# 339
23:32	# 236
26:1	# 237
26:2	# 137
	# 236
	# 283

	# 339
26:6	# 102
	# 284
26:12	# 96—st.3
	# 99
	# 237
26:28	# 349—st.1
26:40	# 237
27:30-33	# 16
	# 350

NUMBERS

6:24	# 208
6:24-26	# 99
6:26	# 73
7:89	# 66—st.1
	# 90
9:15-23	# 96—st.3
9:16	# 210
10:34-35	# 115—st.2
	# 125
11:1-2	# 304—st.3
11:9	# 99—st.2
14:8	# 259
14:11	# 74—st.2
14:18	# 286—st.3
	# 365
14:18-19	# 337
14:19	# 304—st.3
16:30	# 74—st.2
18:21-24	# 16
	# 350
20:2-13	# 115—st.2
21:20	# 307—st.3
23:14	# 307—st.3
24:17	# 131
	# 210
27:17	# 155—st.2
32:12	# 308

DEUTERONOMY

1:11	# 301
3:24	# 138

	# 151
	# 303—st.4
3:27	# 307—st.4
4:22	# 259
4:24	# 210
4:29	# 374—st.4
4:30-31	# 165
4:31	# 74
	# 114
	# 365
4:32	# 38
4:39	# 8
	# 38
	# 63
	# 151
	# 256
	# 270
	# 271
5:12-15	# 236
	# 283
	# 339
5:15	# 102
	# 113
5:16	# 118
	# 243
5:24	# 138
5:29	# 239
6:4	# 132
	# 230—st.3
6:5	# 205
	# 220
	# 224
	# 281—st.1
	# 308
	# 372—st.4
6:6	# 38—st.4
6:6-7	# 212
6:7	# 118
	# 243
6:14	# 318
6:18	# 192—st.3 & 4
	# 198
6:20	# 118
	# 243
6:24	# 51—st.4

7:6	# 11—st.2	**22:21**	# 261		# 51
7:8	# 286	**23:5**	# 69		# 99
7:8-9	# 114	**24:5**	# 250		# 109
7:25	# 237	**24:7**	# 261		# 178
8:2	# 198	**26:7**	# 349		# 199
8:3	# 47	**26:10**	# 350		# 241
	# 99—st.3	**26:12-15**	# 16	**33:27-28**	# 73
	# 194		# 350	**33:29**	# 241
	# 310—st.1	**26:18**	# 301		# 349
8:5	# 349—st.1	**27:3**	# 301	**34:1**	# 307—st.3
8:15	# 282	**27:16**	# 118		

8:16	# 115—st.1		# 243	**1:5**	# 137
8:18	# 93	**28:65**	# 214—st.1		# 158—st.3
9:7	# 74	**29:29**	# 159	**1:9**	# 109
9:29	# 115—st.1	**30:2**	# 308	**2:11**	# 256
10:9	# 301	**30:8**	# 265—st.2		# 270
10:12-13	# 299	**30:15**	# 261	**3:1-17**	# 115—st.3
10:14	# 256	**30:19**	# 261	**3:10**	# 99
	# 331	**31:6**	# 104	**4:6**	# 64—st.2
10:17	# 191		# 137	**4:24**	# 102
11:1	# 224	**31:8**	# 109		# 107
11:13	# 281—st.1		# 137		# 113
	# 372—st.4		# 158	**5:6**	# 170—st.1
11:16	# 237		# 162	**8:1**	# 109
12:6	# 16		# 198	**10:25**	# 109
	# 350		# 264—st.1		# 137—st.2
12:17-19	# 16		# 349	**14:8**	# 308
	# 350	**31:20**	# 74—st.2	**21:44**	# 105
12:20	# 301	**32:3**	# 132	**21:45**	# 114
13:4	# 281		# 151	**22:4**	# 301
	# 299		# 292	**23:5**	# 301
13:5	# 261		# 318	**23:6**	# 127
14:1	# 37—st.2		# 380	**23:10**	# 301
	# 51	**32:4**	# 37	**23:14**	# 114
14:22-29	# 16		# 38—st.4	**23:15**	# 301
	# 350		# 89	**24:14**	# 237
15:6	# 301		# 159—st.2	**24:15**	# 1
15:11	# 161		# 282		# 118
	# 232	**32:5-6**	# 114		# 243
16:22	# 237	**32:10**	# 125		# 250
17:7	# 261	**32:11-12**	# 109—st.1		# 261
19:8	# 301	**32:12**	# 198		# 375
19:19	# 261	**32:43**	# 365	**24:17**	# 51
21:8	# 365	**33:25**	# 71	**24:27**	# 64—st.2
21:21	# 261	**33:27**	# 3		

JUDGES

1:22	# 227—st.4
2:1	# 301
	# 329—st.3
2:9	# 237
5:2	# 308
5:3	# 203
	# 292
	# 353
5:31	# 128

RUTH

2:12	# 9—st.4
	# 99—st.2
	# 109
	# 296—st.1
4:15	# 51—st.2

1 SAMUEL

1:27	# 274
	# 307
	# 360
2:1	# 277
2:2	# 132
	# 158—st.1
2:3	# 101
3:9	# 265
4:1	# 64—st.2
5:1	# 64—st.2
6:20	# 132
7:3	# 237
	# 239
7:12	# 64—st.2
12:11	# 211
12:23	# 192—st. 3 & 4
	# 198
	# 241
14:36	# 141
15:22	# 212
	# 369
	# 374—st.2
16:7	# 205—refrain
	# 239
17:11	# 109

2 SAMUEL

5:7	# 96
7:14	# 37—st.2
	# 349—st.1
7:22	# 230—st.3
7:28	# 38—st.4
	# 89
	# 107
	# 301
7:29	# 69
8:6	# 51—st.4
22:2-4	# 3
	# 37—st.3
	# 282
22:3	# 51
22:7	# 43—st.3
	# 55—st.2
22:7-18	# 3
	# 103
	# 107
22:17	# 137
22:26	# 365
22:29	# 43—st.3
	# 102
	# 125
	# 190
	# 210
	# 248—st.2
	# 296—st.1
	# 347
22:31	# 3
	# 37
22:33	# 102
	# 137
	# 158
22:47	# 158—st.1
22:50	# 68
	# 230
	# 352
23:4	# 32
	# 296—st.1
	# 327
	# 348

23:5	# 114
24:14	# 365

1 KINGS

2:4	# 237
3:14	# 102—st.2
4:20	# 185—st.4
5:12	# 301
8:1	# 96
8:12-13	# 16
8:15	# 114
8:20-25	# 301
8:23	# 101
	# 237
	# 365
8:23-24	# 114
8:27	# 302
8:27-30	# 16
8:56	# 38—st.4
	# 51
	# 107
	# 114
	# 270
	# 301
8:57	# 81
	# 105
	# 191
8:59	# 115
8:61	# 198
	# 239
9:5	# 301
12:9	# 115
15:12	# 237
18:21	# 242
	# 261
19:9-13	# 73
19:12	# 265—st.2

2 KINGS

2:2	# 227—st.4
3:2	# 237
8:19	# 301
13:23	# 114
	# 270
	# 337

15:35	# 267	16:24-31	# 257			# 230
17:28	# 227—st.4	16:25	# 201			# 352
17:29	# 237	16:25-36	# 292	28:20		# 3
19:15	# 8	16:26	# 8			# 109
	# 256		# 237			# 114
20:3	# 237	16:29	# 1—st.1			# 137
23:3	# 237		# 43	29:5		# 308
	# 308	16:29-30	# 100	29:10-13	# 63—st.1	
23:24	# 237	16:31	# 8			# 107
23:25	# 308		# 271			# 256

1 CHRONICLES

			# 273			# 270
			# 331	29:11		# 191
7:11	# 84	16:34	# 39	29:11-13		# 151
	# 197		# 68	29:12		# 102
	# 264		# 74			# 158
16:4	# 230		# 101	29:12-13		# 241
16:8	# 39		# 114	29:13		# 68
	# 68		# 203			# 352
	# 230		# 263—st.1	29:14		# 16
16:9	# 60		# 272			# 350
16:10	# 132		# 365			

2 CHRONICLES

16:23	# 42	16:34-35	# 337			
	# 114	16:34-36	# 230	2:4		# 16
	# 240	16:36	# 299	2:6	# 50—st. 2 & 3	
	# 332—st.1	16:41	# 68	5:13		# 203
	# 351		# 230	6:10		# 301
	# 353		# 352	6:15-16		# 301
16:23-24	# 278	16:41-42	# 60	7:3		# 203
	# 357	17:20	# 230	7:5		# 16
	# 378		# 237	7:14		# 33
16:23-25	# 240	17:26	# 301			# 105
16:23-30	# 201	19:13	# 127			# 274
	# 380	22:13	# 109		# 286—st.3	
16:23-33	# 8		# 127			# 307
	# 13	22:18	# 105			# 360
	# 38	23:25	# 105	13:11		# 1
	# 190	23:30	# 68	15:8		# 237
	# 271		# 72	15:15		# 242
	# 273		# 230	16:7	# 102—st.2	
	# 299		# 299	16:9		# 286
	# 351		# 302	17:16		# 308
	# 353		# 352	19:3		# 239
16:24	# 91		# 353	20:6		# 107
16:24-25	# 39		# 367			# 256
	# 345	25:3	# 68	20:15		# 197

2 CHRONICLES

	# 375	**2:18**	# 113		# 230
20:15-17	# 109	**8:6**	# 38		# 352
20:18	# 100	**8:10**	# 190	**12:40**	# 68
20:21	# 33		# 248—st.3		# 230
	# 89		# 337		# 352
	# 203	**9:5**	# 159	**12:44**	# 16
	# 256		# 299		# 350
	# 272		# 353	**12:46**	# 68
	# 273	**9:6**	# 8		# 230
21:7	# 301		# 11		# 352
29:30	# 38		# 17	**13:5**	# 350
29:31	# 68		# 82	**13:12**	# 350
	# 230		# 108		
	# 352		# 132	**JOB**	
30:8	# 153		# 138		
	# 192		# 151	**1:4-11**	# 105
	# 369		# 207—st.3 & 4	**1:21**	# 51—st.4
30:9	# 293		# 256	**3:17**	# 57—st.3
	# 365		# 271		# 198—st.4
30:21	# 71		# 273	**5:10**	# 352
	# 316	**9:8**	# 239	**5:17**	# 349—st.1
31:5-6	# 350	**9:12**	# 115—st.2	**7:4**	# 193—st.3
31:11-12	# 16	**9:15**	# 296—st.3	**9:4**	# 101
	# 350		# 301		# 159
32:7	# 109	**9:17**	# 74	**9:11**	# 159
33:16	# 68		# 101	**10:1**	# 25
	# 230		# 337	**10:12**	# 286
	# 352		# 365	**11:15**	# 102
		9:19-20	# 115	**12:9**	# 82
EZRA			# 125	**12:9-10**	# 138
		9:20	# 219—st.2		# 256
5:12	# 74—st.2		# 298	**12:13**	# 103
7:9	# 113	**9:21**	# 109		# 159
7:10	# 239	**9:23**	# 301	**12:16**	# 159
7:25	# 37—st.2	**9:27**	# 337	**12:22**	# 306—st.3
8:22	# 159		# 360	**14:10-13**	# 285
8:31	# 211		# 365	**14:14**	# 208—st.3
9:8	# 279	**9:30-31**	# 74	**19:25**	# 126
9:9	# 3	**9:31**	# 365		# 144
	# 114	**10:37-39**	# 16		# 353
9:13	# 365		# 350	**19:25-27**	# 145
9:15	# 107—st.3	**12:31**	# 68		# 302—st.4
			# 230		# 304
NEHEMIAH			# 352		# 324
		12:38	# 68	**20:5**	# 220—st.3
1:4-11	# 105				
1:10	# 353				

22:21	# 284	**40:19**	# 51—st.2	**4:7**	# 108
22:22	# 83	**41:11**	# 256		# 190
22:23	# 261	**41:21**	# 210	**4:8**	# 4
22:26	# 273	**PSALMS**			# 14
23:8-9	# 159				# 72
23:12	# 310—st.1	**1**	# 125		# 199
25:2	# 256	**1:1**	# 29		# 231
26:7	# 8	**1:1-3**	# 195		# 241
	# 151	**1:2**	# 83		# 268
28	# 101		# 377		# 284
	# 103	**1:3**	# 13		# 285
28:28	# 104	**2**	# 65		# 294
	# 261	**2:2**	# 117		# 316
32:8	# 48	**2:6**	# 96	**5**	# 337
	# 298	**2:10-12**	# 13	**5:3**	# 32
33:4	# 38	**2:11**	# 299—st.1		# 59
	# 48	**3**	# 3		# 274
	# 298		# 59		# 302
	# 303—st.2	**3:5**	# 106		# 307
33:19	# 349—st.1		# 231		# 360
34:12	# 159—st.2		# 284		# 367
34:19	# 338		# 302	**5:7**	# 100
34:28	# 286	**3:8**	# 69		# 101
34:29	# 73		# 102		# 200
36:5	# 159		# 349		# 214
36:19	# 69—st.3	**4:1**	# 286—st.2		# 299
36:22-23	# 103	**4:3**	# 286—st.2		# 337
36:26	# 241	**4:3-5**	# 353	**5:8**	# 115
37	# 107	**4:4**	# 73		# 125
37:9-13	# 256—st.3		# 285		# 198
37:14	# 69		# 294	**5:11**	# 175
37:14-24	# 8		# 316		# 190
	# 101	**4:5**	# 36		# 276
	# 103		# 103		# 349
	# 159		# 158	**5:12**	# 337
37:24	# 195		# 263	**6:2**	# 115—st.1
38:4-7	# 338		# 369		# 365
38:7	# 20—st.1	**4:5-8**	# 102	**6:5**	# 68
	# 49	**4:6**	# 43—st.3		# 230
	# 190—st.4		# 159		# 352
	# 247—st.2		# 210	**6:9**	# 274
38:8-11	# 77—st.1		# 248—st.2		# 307
38:12	# 32		# 296—st.1		# 360
			# 367	**7:1**	# 36
38:41	# 296—st.3	**4:6-8**	# 304		# 346

	# 167	**19:2**	# 316		# 91
	# 263	**19:6**	# 182—st.1	**22:28-31**	# 63
	# 346	**19:7-8**	# 45		# 256
18:6	# 55—st.2		# 83	**23**	# 13
	# 286—st.2		# 194		# 109
18:16	# 137		# 213		# 115
18:25	# 107		# 304		# 125
	# 159—st.2	**19:9-10**	# 69		# 162
18:28	# 43—st.3	**19:12**	# 57		# 286
	# 67—st.2		# 193		# 289
	# 102		# 286—st.3		# 306
	# 155—st.4		# 335		# 322
	# 159		# 374		# 325
	# 184—st.4	**19:14**	# 212	**23:1-2**	# 286—st.1
	# 210		# 282	**23:2**	# 25
	# 244—st.3	**20:1**	# 349		# 73
	# 296—st.1	**20:4-5**	# 272		# 150
	# 304		# 277	**23:2-3**	# 26
	# 358—st.3	**20:5**	# 85		# 198
18:30	# 3		# 264—st.1	**23:3**	# 84—st.2
	# 195		# 300—st.1		# 279
18:31	# 158	**20:7**	# 36		# 286—st.2
	# 282		# 175		# 289—st.4
18:32	# 99		# 238	**23:4**	# 4
18:46	# 41		# 263		# 22
	# 89		# 346		# 208—st.3
18:48	# 211	**21:4**	# 102—st.2		# 218
18:49	# 68	**21:13**	# 107		# 226
	# 230		# 159	**23:5**	# 289—st.3
	# 352		# 201	**23:6**	# 13—st.4
19	# 8		# 256		# 114
	# 273		# 271		# 155—st.5
	# 321		# 272		# 169
19:1	# 8		# 292		# 170
	# 39—st.2		# 318		# 178
	# 138		# 353		# 259
	# 151	**22**	# 3		# 273—st.3
	# 190—st.2	**22:3**	# 132		# 302—st.4
	# 338		# 318		# 365
19:1-2	# 72	**22:3-5**	# 105		*# 368
19:1-6	# 87	**22:4-5**	# 81	**24**	# 8
	# 331		# 86		# 63
19:1-8	# 17	**22:22-31**	# 299		# 204
	# 132—st.4	**22:23**	# 318		# 256
19:1-10	# 114—st.2	**22:27**	# 54		# 273

PSALMS

	# 277		# 263	**28:2**	# 108
24:1	# 8		# 346	**28:7**	# 3
	# 338	**26:2**	# 122—st.2		# 36
24:1-6	# 108	**26:3**	# 33		# 95
24:7	# 267		# 89—st.2		# 115
	# 341		# 198—st.2		# 158
24:7-10	# 204		# 347		# 167
24:8	# 3		# 365		# 190—st.2
	# 107	**26:7**	# 39		# 292
	# 159		# 68		# 346
25	# 211		# 138	**28:7-8**	# 137
	# 256		# 272	**28:8**	# 102
25:1-5	# 211		# 352		# 180—st.1
25:2	# 36	**26:8**	# 148	**28:9**	# 325
	# 167		# 322—st.5	**29**	# 107
	# 238	**27**	# 36		# 159
	# 263		# 95		# 190
	# 346		# 167		# 273
25:3	# 171		# 238	**29:2**	# 63
25:4	# 198	**27:1**	# 71		# 100
25:4-5	# 125		# 101		# 345
25:5	# 32		# 159	**29:4**	# 151
25:6	# 15		# 175—st.1	**29:10**	# 38
	# 203		# 211		# 82
	# 365		# 304		# 230—st.3
25:6-7	# 33		# 306		# 316
25:7	# 209	**27:1-3**	# 102	**29:11**	# 102
25:8	# 322		# 295—st.2		# 150
25:8-10	# 125		# 375		# 175—st.1
25:9	# 158	**27:3**	# 90		# 198—st.1
25:9-10	# 198	**27:4**	# 108		# 211
25:10	# 33		# 267		# 268
	# 84—st.2		# 322—st.5		# 284
	# 306	**27:4-7**	# 115	**30:4**	# 60
25:11	# 178—st.4	**27:5**	# 51		# 68
	# 244—st.2		# 123		# 131
25:14	# 200		# 241		# 132
25:19-20	# 211	**27:7**	# 365		# 201
25:20	# 36	**27:8**	# 239		# 292
	# 167	**27:9**	# 158—st.3		# 318
	# 263	**27:11**	# 125		# 380—st.1
	# 346		# 158	**30:4-5**	# 14
25:21	# 51—st.4		# 198	**30:5**	# 4
26:1	# 167	**28**	# 107		# 32
	# 238	**28:1**	# 282		# 33

PSALMS

Ref	Hymn	Ref	Hymn	Ref	Hymn
	# 337		# 178		# 39
	# 365		# 211	**40:17**	# 109
36:5-6	# 107	**37:39-40**	# 273		# 158
36:6	# 159—st.2	**38:4**	# 147		# 165
36:7	# 3	**38:9**	# 26		# 209
	# 33	**38:15**	# 26		# 218
	# 99—st.2		# 241	**41:13**	# 39
	# 109		# 329		# 270
	# 273—st.2	**39:7**	# 26		# 292
	# 296—st.1		# 241		# 318
36:9	# 43—st.3		# 329	**42**	# 3
	# 102	**39:12**	# 52		# 26
	# 210		# 127		# 273
	# 248—st.2	**40**	# 190	**42:1**	# 150
	# 296—st.1	**40:1**	# 310	**42:1-2**	# 26
	# 305	**40:1-5**	# 103	**42:5**	# 26
	# 347		# 256—st.4		# 69—st.1
36:9-10	# 195		# 353		# 292
	# 323	**40:2**	# 163	**42:7-8**	# 33
	# 333		# 329	**42:7-11**	# 165
37:3-5	# 36	**40:3**	# 41—refrain	**42:8**	# 14
	# 167		# 54		# 32
	# 238		# 240		# 106
	# 346		# 269		# 294
	# 369		# 356		# 316
37:3-7	# 263		# 380	**42:9**	# 26
37:4-5	# 109	**40:3-4**	# 263	**42:11**	# 26
	# 256—st.4	**40:4**	# 369	**43**	# 3
	# 273—st.2	**40:5**	# 69		# 39
37:5	# 95		# 138	**43:3**	# 101
	# 158	**40:7**	# 308		# 192—st.3
	# 344	**40:8**	# 76		# 195
37:11	# 284		# 83		# 198
37:17	# 109		# 122	**43:5**	# 26
37:23	# 198		# 141—st.2		# 69—st.1
	# 306		# 194		# 241
37:24	# 113		# 212		# 273
	# 137—st.2		# 213	**44:1-3**	# 105
37:28	# 51—st.4		# 219—st.2	**44:4**	# 63—st.1
	# 55—st.3		# 223	**44:4-7**	# 256
	# 101		# 265	**44:5**	# 80
	# 107		# 286—st.4		# 211
	# 301		# 303—st.3	**44:8**	# 105
37:29	# 175	**40:10**	# 351		# 171
37:39	# 102	**40:10-11**	# 33	**44:26**	# 101

PSALMS

51:17	# 237	**56:13**	# 237	**61:2**	# 125
52:1	# 203		# 347		# 282
	# 322	**57:1**	# 9—st.4	**61:3**	# 102
	# 365		# 77		# 211
52:8	# 167		# 99—st.2	**61:5**	# 192—st.2
	# 263		# 109	**61:8**	# 32
	# 365		# 124—st.3		# 60
52:8-9	# 101		# 165		# 131
	# 107		# 191—st.1		# 132
	# 114		# 195		# 201
	# 256—st.4		# 273—st.2		# 273
52:9	# 203—st.2		# 360		# 353
54	# 3	**57:3**	# 102—st.2		# 356
55	# 3		# 114	**62:1-2**	# 211
	# 158	**57:5**	# 107	**62:1-8**	# 3
55:1	# 274		# 151		# 282
	# 307	**57:7**	# 239	**62:2**	# 158
	# 360	**57:8**	# 32	**62:5-8**	# 211
55:8	# 378—st.2	**57:9**	# 380—st.1	**62:8**	# 36
55:14	# 43	**57:10**	# 33		# 153
55:17	# 14		# 107—st.2		# 167
	# 274		# 114—st.2		# 238
	# 307	**58**	# 107		# 310
	# 316		# 159—st.2		# 346
	# 360	**58:11**	# 191	**62:11**	# 151
55:22	# 25	**59**	# 3	**62:11-12**	# 132
	# 69—st.2	**59:1-2**	# 211	**62:12**	# 33
	# 71	**59:10**	# 114	**63:1**	# 26
	# 109	**59:13**	# 131		# 40
	# 158		# 256	**63:2**	# 273—st.1
	# 165	**59:16**	# 151	**63:3**	# 33
	# 175		# 302		# 89
	# 238	**59:16-17**	# 256		# 203
	# 307		# 338		# 292
	# 324		# 367		# 365
	# 360	**59:17**	# 292	**63:3-5**	# 201
	# 361—st.4	**60:1-3**	# 103	**63:4**	# 87—st.4
56:3-4	# 36	**60:4**	# 99—st.4		# 299
	# 95		# 85	**63:5**	# 89
	# 103		# 255		# 152—st.5
	# 256—st.4		# 300—st.1		# 190
	# 346	**60:6**	# 132		# 230
	# 369—st.4	**60:12**	# 127	**63:6**	# 14
56:4	# 71	**61:1-4**	# 3		# 316
	# 90		# 273	**63:6-8**	# 231

	# 284	**66:4**	# 201		# 271
	# 285	**66:7**	# 151	**70**	# 3
	# 294	**66:9**	# 102	**70:4**	# 102
63:7	# 9—st.4	**66:13-14**	# 192—st.2	**71:1**	# 36
	# 99—st.2	**66:16**	# 149		# 167
	# 273—st.2		# 163		# 238
63:8	# 99	**67**	# 91		# 263
63:11	# 277		# 107		# 346
64:2	# 51		# 182		# 369
	# 241—st.2		# 256	**71:1-8**	# 3
64:10	# 277		# 272	**71:1-16**	# 211
65	# 272	**67:1-2**	# 104	**71:3**	# 51
65:1	# 96	**67:2**	# 257		# 102
65:2	# 274		# 278		# 282
	# 307		# 351	**71:3-5**	# 241
	# 360		# 357	**71:5**	# 26
65:3	# 108—st.2		# 378		# 192—st.1
	# 122—st.2	**67:3**	# 131		# 329
	# 140—st.2	**67:3-5**	# 60	**71:6-8**	# 256
	# 191		# 201		# 292
	# 263		# 292		# 353
	# 286—st.3	**67:4**	# 356	**71:6-9**	# 277—st.3
	# 344—st.2	**67:5**	# 131	**71:7**	# 102
65:4	# 11—st.2		# 353—st.3	**71:9**	# 158—st.3
	# 322—st.5	**68**	# 105	**71:14**	# 26—st.4
65:4-13	# 69	**68:3-4**	# 277		# 60
65:5	# 296	**68:4**	# 292		# 329
65:5-8	# 72	**68:5**	# 107	**71:14-16**	# 52
65:6	# 151		# 132	**71:15**	# 351
65:7	# 103	**68:10**	# 64	**71:16**	# 299—st.4
	# 181	**68:19**	# 64	**71:18**	# 277—st.2
65:9-11	# 68		# 68	**71:21**	# 365
	# 352		# 203	**71:22**	# 318
65:11	# 113		# 352	**71:22-24**	# 107
66	# 270		# 353		# 114
	# 272	**68:32**	# 201		# 270
66:1	# 11—st.3	**69:3**	# 168—st.4		# 353
66:1-2	# 42	**69:16**	# 33	**71:23**	# 38—st.3
	# 201		# 107—st.2		# 42
	# 269		# 203		#240
66:1-4	# 240	**69:30**	# 68		# 269
66:2	# 60		# 230	**72**	# 107
	# 183—st.2		# 352		# 117
	# 244	**69:34**	# 72		# 182
	# 356		# 201	**72:7**	# 284

PSALMS

Reference	Hymn
72:8	# 181
72:10-11	# 20
	# 27
	# 65
	# 317—st.3
72:11	# 11—st.3
	# 81
	# 131
72:18-19	# 345
73:1	# 277
73:23	# 69—st.4
73:23-24	# 99
	# 115
	# 125
	# 195
	# 285
	# 302
73:23-28	# 4
73:24	# 52
	# 113—st.2
	# 222—st.3 & 4
	# 253
73:25	# 26
73:26	# 102
	# 137
	# 158
	# 180—st.1
	# 205—refrain
73:27	# 3
	# 107
73:28	# 71
	# 76
	# 141
	# 150
	# 167
	# 222
	# 226
	# 227
	# 310
	# 346
	# 369
74	# 3
74:12	# 256
74:16	# 8
	# 32

Reference	Hymn
	# 190
	# 304
	# 316
	# 367—st.3
75	# 107
75:1	# 68
	# 230
75:7	# 191
76	# 107
77:3	# 138
77:6	# 316
77:8	# 301
77:9	# 349—st.1
77:13	# 100
	# 132
	# 303
77:14	# 105
	# 107
77:19-20	# 103
77:20	# 52
	# 115
	# 125
	# 286
	# 289
	# 322
	# 325
78	# 107
78:7	# 329
78:14-16	# 115—st.2
	# 195
78:20	# 109—st.3
78:26	# 107
78:35	# 256
	# 282
	# 329
	# 353
78:40	# 74—st.2
78:52	# 115
	# 125
	# 325
78:53	# 199
78:56	# 74—st.2
79:8	# 178—st.4
79:9	# 191
	# 286—st.3

Reference	Hymn
79:11	# 107
79:13	# 38—st.2
	# 68
	# 99—st.1
	# 201
	# 230
	# 286
	# 292
	# 322—st.5
	# 352
80:1	# 115
	# 125
	# 289
	# 322
	# 325
80:3	# 108
	# 286—st.3
80:7	# 108
80:19	# 108
81:1	# 60
	# 318
81:1-3	# 39
	# 190
	# 273
81:9	# 237
82	# 107
	# 159—st.2
	# 326
82:5	# 227—st.2
	# 347
82:8	# 115
	# 326—st.3
	# 338
83	# 107
83:1	# 214—st.3
83:18	# 38
	# 63—st.1
	# 151
	# 256
84	# 256
	# 273
84:1-4	# 100
84:2	# 64—st.3
	# 239
	# 322—st.5

PSALMS

Ref	Hymn	Ref	Hymn	Ref	Hymn
92:3-4	# 190		# 299	**98**	# 8
92:8	# 270		# 351		# 107
92:15	# 114		# 353		# 189
93	# 114	**96:1**	# 356		# 190
	# 132	**96:1-2**	# 42		# 256
	# 256		# 114		# 353
	# 270		# 240	**98:3-4**	# 13
	# 273		# 332—st.1	**98:4**	# 89
93:1	# 38	**96:1-4**	# 240	**98:8-9**	# 326—st.2
	# 151	**96:1-9**	# 201	**98:9**	# 191
93:4	# 151	**96:1-10**	# 380		# 337
94	# 107	**96:2-3**	# 278	**99**	# 107
94:11	# 103		# 357		# 273
94:15	# 277		# 378	**99:2**	# 96
94:17	# 102	**96:3**	# 91	**99:3**	# 292
	# 158	**96:3-4**	# 39		# 318
94:19	# 324		# 345	**99:5**	# 100
94:22	# 3	**96:3-10**	# 257	**99:9**	# 131
	# 158	**96:5**	# 8		# 292
	# 282	**96:8-9**	# 1—st.1	**100**	# 13
95:1	# 356		# 43		# 38
95:1-2	# 60	**96:9**	# 100		# 190
95:1-6	# 273	**96:10**	# 91		# 270
	# 353		# 278		# 273
95:2	# 230		# 357		# 299
95:3	# 138	**96:13**	# 191		# 353
	# 326—st.4		# 326—st.2	**100:1**	# 39
95:3-5	# 8	**97**	# 8	**100:2**	# 60
	# 63		# 13		# 356
	# 256		# 63	**100:3**	# 286
95:3-6	# 151		# 107	**100:4**	# 68
95:5	# 77		# 159		# 230
95:6	# 43		# 256	**100:5**	# 33
95:7	# 99—st.1		# 273		# 102—st.2
	# 162	**97:1**	# 151		# 114
	# 322		# 292		# 184—st.2
	# 325	**97:6**	# 138		# 203
95:8	# 341	**97:10**	# 51—st.4	**101:1**	# 33
96	# 8		# 104—st.2		# 107
	# 13		# 261	**101:2**	# 118
	# 38	**97:11**	# 128		# 195
	# 190	**97:12**	# 68		# 243
	# 271		# 230	**102:11-12**	# 270
	# 273		# 292	**102:11-21**	# 114
	# 292		# 352	**102:18**	# 45

PSALMS

107:9	# 109—st.3	**111**	# 114	**116:6**	# 51—st.4
	# 123—st.3		# 270		# 346
	# 184		# 271	**116:7**	# 25
	# 291—st.2		# 273		# 226
107:10	# 306—st.3		# 353	**116:9**	# 237
107:14	# 162—st.3	**111:3**	# 4—st.2	**116:12**	# 64
107:15	# 33		# 185		# 142
107:21	# 33	**111:5**	# 301	**116:13**	# 296—st.2
107:21-22	# 87	**111:7**	# 38—st.4	**116:15**	# 208—st.3
107:22	# 68	**111:9**	# 132		# 322
	# 230		# 361—st.1	**116:17**	# 68
	# 272	**112**	# 101		# 230
	# 277		# 103		# 352
	# 299		# 107	**117**	# 8
	# 352		# 190		# 33
107:23-32	# 77	**112:4**	# 184—st.4		# 63
107:28-30	# 181		# 244—st.3		# 89
	# 187—st.4	**112:6**	# 209		# 114
107:29	# 36—st.2	**112:7**	# 95		# 273
	# 90		# 104—st.2		# 292
	# 103—st.1		# 153	**117:1**	# 201
	# 378		# 158	**117:2**	# 203
107:31	# 33		# 296	**118**	# 256
107:32	# 299		# 369—st.4		# 273
107:38	# 69	**112:7-8**	# 36		# 339
107:41	# 93	**113**	# 273	**118:1**	# 68
107:43	# 33	**113:1-2**	# 318		# 230
108	# 3	**113:1-3**	# 272	**118:1-4**	# 33
108:1-4	# 33	**113:2-3**	# 316		# 89—st.2
	# 59	**113:3**	# 131		# 203
	# 107		# 201	**118:6**	# 199
	# 190	**113:4**	# 256	**118:8**	# 36
	# 367	**115**	# 273		# 102
108:2-3	# 32	**115:1**	# 13		# 153
108:4	# 74		# 299		# 157
	# 84—st.3		# 353		# 222
	# 365	**115:3**	# 271		# 238
108:13	# 127	**115:9**	# 241		# 263
109	# 3	**115:9-11**	# 3		# 310
	# 33		# 256—st.4		# 344
	# 214—st.3	**115:11**	# 158—st.3		# 369
109:22	# 54	**116**	# 107	**118:8-9**	# 175
	# 266		# 337		# 346
109:23	# 193—st.3	**116:1-9**	# 218	**118:14**	# 211
110	# 270	**116:3**	# 165—st.3	**118:15**	# 137—st.2

118:18	# 349—st.1		# 255	**119:92**	# 83
118:19-20	# 267	**119:24-25**	# 321—st.4		# 377
118:21	# 353	**119:28**	# 45—st.1	**119:97**	# 83
118:22	# 28—st.2	**119:30**	# 192	**119:100**	# 194
	# 50		# 194	**119:104**	# 194—st.4
	# 55		# 198—st.2		# 303
	# 282		# 261	**119:105**	# 45—st.1
	# 314	**119:33**	# 47—st.3		# 83
118:24	# 236		# 83		# 137—st.1
	# 283		# 194		# 194
	# 339		# 213		# 213
118:27	# 159	**119:33-34**	# 122		# 255—st.1
	# 210	**119:34**	# 308	**119:114**	# 139—st.3
118:28-29	# 292	**119:35**	# 84—st.2		# 241
118:29	# 203		# 198	**119:116**	# 241
	# 230	**119:41**	# 83		# 329
	# 352	**119:45**	# 45—st.1	**119:128**	# 321—st.4
119	# 45		# 47—st.2	**119:128-130**	# 213
	# 47	**119:49**	# 321	**119:129**	# 377
	# 54—st.2	**119:49-50**	# 39—st.2	**119:130**	# 45—st.1
	# 83		# 146—st.2		# 83
	# 255		# 324—st.3		# 342
	# 271	**119:58**	# 39—st.2	**119:131**	# 26
	# 321	**119:62**	# 68	**119:133-134**	# 211
	# 377	**119:64**	# 33	**119:134**	# 349
119:2	# 239		# 47—st.3	**119:137**	# 107
119:7-8	# 106—st.2		# 84—st.3	**119:140**	# 83
119:9	# 192—st.1 & 2		# 337	**119:142**	# 47—
	# 213	**119:66**	# 47—st.3		st.2 & 3
	# 321—st.4	**119:66-67**	# 194		# 107
119:11	# 194	**119:68**	# 322	**119:147**	# 302
119:12	# 47—st.3	**119:69**	# 308	**119:148**	# 294
	# 83	**119:70**	# 83	**119:149**	# 33
119:12-13	# 212	**119:74**	# 377	**119:151**	# 71
119:16	# 83	**119:76**	# 33		# 141
	# 213		# 324	**119:156**	# 107—st.2
119:17-20	# 106—st.2	**119:76-77**	# 83		# 203
119:18	# 265	**119:77**	# 365	**119:159**	# 83
119:18-20	# 47—st.3	**119:81**	# 47		# 321
	# 83		# 83		# 377
	# 213		# 146—st.2	**119:160**	# 45
119:19	# 52		# 377		# 255
119:20	# 26	**119:89**	# 145—st.2	**119:161**	# 321
119:24	# 83		# 321	**119:161-163**	# 83
	# 194	**119:90-91**	# 114	**119:165**	# 83

PSALMS

	# 211	127:2	# 14		# 273
	# 213		# 231		# 318
	# 268	127:3	# 118	135:3	# 203
	# 377—st.3		# 243	135:5-6	# 151
119:166	# 329	128	# 190—st.3	135:13	# 241
119:167	# 377		# 270—st.2	136	# 33
119:171	# 201		# 272		# 39
119:172	# 377	128:1	# 355—st.3		# 89—st.2
119:173	# 261	128:5	# 96		# 101
119:174	# 83		# 267		# 114
	# 102	130:2	# 274		# 203
119:176	# 64—st.3		# 307		# 214
	# 155—st.2		# 360		# 337
	# 322—st.3	130:5	# 310	136:1-2	# 203
120	# 214—st.3	130:6	# 32	136:1-9	# 8
121	# 3		# 231	136:3-9	# 17
	# 13		# 316	136:3-26	# 107—st.2
	# 109		# 348	136:7	# 203
	# 115—st.2	130:7	# 183—st.3	136:25	# 296—st.3
	# 158		# 241		# 352
	# 256—st.1		# 286—st.3	136:25-26	# 203
121:3-4	# 114		# 291	137:5-6	# 148
121:4	# 292—st.2		# 329	138	# 214—st.3
121:5	# 162		# 365	138:1	# 239
	# 178	130:7-8	# 269—st.2		# 299
121:7	# 106	131	# 73	138:2	# 33
122:2	# 170		# 103		# 83
122:4	# 68		# 256—st.4		# 107
123	# 337	132	# 20—st.4		# 256
123:3	# 365	132:10-12	# 373—st.3		# 321
124	# 39	132:13	# 96	138:3	# 18—st.1
	# 256		# 267	138:5	# 292
124:8	# 17	133:1	# 44		# 345
125	# 103—st.3		# 87—st.3	138:7	# 279
	# 256—st.4		# 161		# 324
125:1	# 96		# 188	138:8	# 337
125:2	# 4		# 232		# 365
	# 71		# 264—st.3	139:1-12	# 101
126	# 105		# 375		# 105
126:1-2	# 96	133:2	# 87		# 115
126:2-3	# 345	134	# 273		# 125
127:1	# 118		# 299		# 302
	# 243	134:1	# 316		# 325
	# 250	135	# 195		# 353
	# 348		# 270	139:3	# 198

139:7	# 226		# 263	**145:3**	# 107
	# 292—st.3		# 346		# 151
139:7-10	# 160	**142**	# 3		# 201
139:7-12	# 4	**142:1**	# 101		# 303
139:8	# 36		# 337	**145:5**	# 294
139:9-10	# 32	**143:1**	# 114	**145:6**	# 151
	# 33—st.3	**143:2**	# 37	**145:7**	# 203
	# 102	**143:5**	# 105		# 322
	# 286	**143:6**	# 26	**145:7-9**	# 365
139:9-11	# 198	**143:8**	# 36	**145:8-9**	# 125
139:11	# 162—st.3		# 238		# 325
			# 302		# 337
139:11-12	# 14		# 346	**145:9**	# 203
	# 101	**143:8-10**	# 115	**145:10**	# 190—st.2
	# 128—st.2		# 125	**145:10-12**	# 151
	# 184—st.4		# 369	**145:10-13**	# 8
	# 231	**143:9**	# 51		# 63
	# 244—st.3	**143:10**	# 76		# 125
	# 285		# 122		# 271
	# 304		# 141—st.2		# 338
	# 367—st.3		# 192	**145:13**	# 67—st.3
139:14	# 138		# 212—st.2		# 82
139:17	# 209		# 219—st.2		# 182
139:17-18	# 69		# 223		# 270
	# 106		# 286—st.4		# 276
	# 302		# 310—st.4		# 316
139:24	# 115	**143:11**	# 345		# 318
	# 306	**143:12**	# 33		# 349—st.2
140	# 214—st.3	**144:1-2**	# 3	**145:14**	# 114
140:1	# 211	**144:15**	# 242	**145:14-21**	# 175
140:13	# 4—st.3		# 356	**145:15**	# 203
	# 68	**145**	# 39	**145:17-20**	# 107
	# 230		# 132		# 337
	# 267		# 190	**145:18**	# 4
	# 272		# 256		# 25
	# 292		# 273		# 71
141:2	# 285		# 292		# 76
	# 294	**145:1-2**	# 19—st.4		# 141
	# 316		# 60		# 222—st.3
141:3	# 212		# 276		# 226
141:8	# 3		# 299—st.5		# 227
	# 36		# 353	**145:18-20**	# 150
	# 167	**145:1-13**	# 138	**145:21**	# 11—st.3
	# 238	**145:2**	# 32		# 38
					# 42

PSALMS

Reference	Hymn
	# 89
	# 131
	# 201
	# 271
	# 380
146	# 17
	# 107
	# 256
	# 270
	# 292
146:5	# 241
	# 329
146:6	# 38—st.4
	# 89
146:8	# 193—st.4
	# 240—st.3
146:10	# 82
	# 241—st.3
	# 318
147	# 107
	# 159
	# 271
	# 272
	# 273
	# 292
	# 299
147:1	# 277
	# 367—st.2
147:3	# 122—st.3
	# 155
	# 178—st.3
147:7	# 68
	# 230
	# 277
	# 352
147:11	# 365
147:12	# 96
	# 356
147:12-15	# 105
147:15	# 45—st.2 & 3
147:19	# 45—st.2 & 3
148	# 8
	# 72
	# 131
	# 132—st.4
	# 190—st.2
	# 201
	# 271
	# 292
	# 331
	# 367—st.4
148:2	# 11
	# 119—st.1
	# 207—st.2 & 3
	# 269
	# 270—st.4
148:5	# 11
	# 38
	# 89
	# 315—st.3
148:12-13	# 277
148:13	# 37
	# 132
	# 273
148:13-14	# 201
	# 318
149	# 131
	# 190
	# 273
	# 292
	# 345
149:1-2	# 356
149:5	# 54—st.4
	# 60
	# 316
150	# 39
	# 131
	# 190
	# 269
	# 273
	# 292
150:2	# 138
	# 151
150:6	# 8
	# 13
	# 38—st.4
	# 60
	# 89
	# 201
	# 271
	# 367—st.4

PROVERBS

Reference	Hymn
1:2-7	# 104
1:8	# 118
	# 243
1:24	# 246
	# 293
1:33	# 55—st.3
	# 73
	# 102
	# 104—st.2
	# 195
2:3-5	# 37
	# 219
	# 299—st.2
	# 303
2:8	# 51—st.4
	# 55—st.3
	# 109
2:9	# 198
2:13	# 227—st.2
	# 347
3:5	# 36
	# 310—st.3
	# 344
	# 346
3:5-6	# 158
	# 238
3:6	# 124—st.4
	# 162—st.2
	# 198
	# 349
3:9-10	# 68
	# 69
3:10	# 64
3:11-12	# 349—st.1
3:13	# 219
3:19	# 151
	# 159
3:23	# 198
3:23-26	# 199
3:24	# 14
	# 231
3:24-26	# 285

	# 316	**14:16**	# 104	**21:3**	# 374—st.2
3:26	# 71	**14:26**	# 40	**21:10**	# 214—st.2
	# 95		# 51	**21:16**	# 257—st.2
4:1	# 118		# 241	**21:17**	# 165—st.2
	# 243	**14:32**	# 208—st.3	**21:30**	# 103
4:5	# 219		# 257—st.2	**22:1**	# 139
	# 303		# 322—st.4	**22:2**	# 69—st.3
4:11	# 84—st.2		# 329	**22:6**	# 118
	# 198	**14:34**	# 105		# 243
4:14-15	# 261	**15:8**	# 274		# 289—st.1
4:18	# 84—st.2		# 307	**22:9**	# 370
	# 128		# 360	**23:23**	# 303
	# 192—st.3	**15:13**	# 239	**24:16**	# 281
	# 198	**15:14**	# 219	**25:21**	# 270
	# 237	**15:29**	# 55—st.2	**25:25**	# 91
4:19	# 227—st.2		# 286—st.2		# 278
	# 347	**15:31**	# 265—st.2	**27:1**	# 32
4:23	# 239	**16:2**	# 122—st.2		# 113—st.3
4:26	# 308	**16:4**	# 17		# 223—st.3
4:27	# 261		# 107		# 296
8:17	# 183—st.4	**16:6**	# 107	**27:8**	# 64—st.3
	# 286—st.3 & 4	**16:7**	# 102		# 322—st.3
	# 374—st.4		# 211	**28:14**	# 237
8:20	# 107	**16:9**	# 115	**28:20**	# 69
	# 125		# 125	**28:27**	# 370
	# 159—st.2	**16:16**	# 219	**29:7**	# 54
8:23	# 270	**16:18**	# 56—st.3	**29:18**	# 37
10:1	# 118	**16:19**	# 239		# 105
	# 243	**16:20**	# 263—st.3	**29:23**	# 56—st.3
10:12	# 161		# 344	**29:25**	# 198—st.3
10:22	# 69		# 346	**30:4**	# 378—st.2
10:27	# 102—st.2		# 369	**30:5**	# 71
10:28	# 329	**18:10**	# 241		# 178
10:31	# 265—st.3	**18:22**	# 250		# 213
11:2	# 56—st.3	**18:24**	# 157		# 241
11:7	# 257—st.2		# 187—st.1		# 321
11:30	# 278		# 228	**30:6**	# 45—st.3
	# 351		# 360	**31:30**	# 118
	# 357	**19:17**	# 350—st.4		# 243
	# 378	**20:4**	# 352		# 250
12:4	# 250	**20:12**	# 265		
13:10	# 56—st.3	**20:24**	# 103		
	# 335—st.2		# 212	**ECCLESIASTES**	
13:24	# 118		# 286	**2:5**	# 352
14:1	# 250	**20:28**	# 38	**2:13**	# 101

ECCLESIASTES

	# 195
2:23	# 165
2:24-26	# 190
2:26	# 93
3:2	# 352
3:8	# 105
	# 107
3:11	# 17
	# 103
3:14	# 51—st.4
	# 296—st.4
3:17	# 191
5:10	# 69—st.3
	# 308
5:12	# 69—st.3
7:8	# 221—st.3
8:12-13	# 167
9:9	# 250
11:5	# 103
11:6	# 32
	# 352
11:9	# 192—st.1
12:1	# 192—st.1 & 2
	# 277
12:7	# 22
12:13	# 107
	# 299—st.2
12:13-14	# 1—st.3
12:14	# 191

SONG OF SOLOMON

1:3	# 139
2:1	# 79—st.2
	# 324
	# 378
2:4	# 85
	# 99
	# 160
	# 186
	# 248—st.1
	# 300—st.1
	# 364
2:16	# 187—st.5
	# 228

5:10	# 324
5:10-16	# 215
6:4	# 300—st.1
6:10	# 210

ISAIAH

1:2	# 51—st.2
1:18	# 23
	# 42—st.3
	# 57—st.3
	# 111—st.2
	# 147
	# 178—st.4
	# 180
	# 185
	# 193
	# 229
	# 240—st.4
	# 244—st.2
	# 263—st.2
	# 286—st.3
	# 335
	# 344—st.2
	# 374
1:18-19	# 333
1:25	# 137—st.4
2:3	# 198
	# 306
2:5	# 195
	# 304
	# 347
	# 367—st.3
2:8	# 237
2:22	# 256—st.4
4:5	# 96
4:6	# 40
5:20	# 261
6:2-3	# 159
	# 200
	# 236
6:3	# 72
	# 131
	# 318
6:7	# 57—st.3
	# 122—st.2

	# 140—st.2
	# 185
	# 193
	# 335
	# 344—st.2
	# 374
6:8	# 91
	# 121
	# 216
	# 257
	# 278
	# 351
	# 355—st.4
	# 357
	# 372
	# 375
	# 378
7:14	# 20—st.2
	# 94
	# 120
	# 147—st.3
	# 234
	# 247—st.4
	# 262—st.1
	# 290
	# 378—st.1
8:13	# 103—st.2
	# 200
	# 299—st.2
8:20	# 101
	# 195
	# 255
9:2	# 67—st.2
	# 91—st.3
	# 128
	# 143—st.3
	# 162—st.3
	# 210
	# 222—st.3
	# 247
	# 248—st.2
	# 305
	# 315—st.2
	# 323
	# 342

ISAIAH

	# 71	33:17	# 259		# 139—st.4
	# 143—st.1	33:20-21	# 96		# 162
28:16	# 28—st.2	33:22	# 63		# 178
	# 50		# 107		# 269—st.1
	# 55		# 159—st.3		# 286
	# 64—st.2		# 191		# 289
	# 137		# 256		# 306
	# 139—st.3	34:4	# 167—st.4		# 322
	# 282	34:16	# 255		# 325
28:24	# 352	35:8	# 310	40:12	# 8
28:29	# 101	35:10	# 3	40:26	# 105
	# 113—st.2		# 15—st.3		# 210
29:16	# 122		# 41		# 325
29:18	# 193—st.4		# 52		# 331
	# 265		# 54—st.4	40:26-31	# 3
	# 358—st.3		# 60—st.3		# 17
30:15	# 25		# 78		# 103
	# 26		# 152—st.4 & 5		# 159
	# 71		# 154	40:28	# 4—st.2
	# 73		# 155		# 82
	# 226		# 168—st.4		# 151
	# 296		# 169		# 296—st.4
30:18	# 286—st.3		# 170	40:29	# 102
	# 310		# 190		# 175—st.1
30:21-22	# 355—st.3		# 217—st.4		# 361—st.4
31:2	# 107		# 220—st.3 & 4	40:31	# 76—st.2
	# 159		# 222—st.3 & 4		# 90—last st.
31:5	# 349		# 240—st.3	41:8-9	# 11—st.2
32:2	# 25		# 242	41:10	# 71
	# 26		# 244—st.4		# 76
	# 40		# 253		# 90
	# 51		# 259		# 95
	# 90		# 275		# 104
	# 178		# 291		# 124—st.1
	# 199		# 313		# 137—st.2
	# 241		# 356		# 158
	# 266		# 368		# 165
	# 300—st.1	38:19	# 118		# 175
	# 378—st.2		# 243		# 178—st.3
32:17	# 36	40:3-5	# 189	41:13	# 69—st.4
	# 73	40:4	# 78—st.3	41:13-14	# 103—st.2
	# 226	40:8	# 255		# 125
32:17-18	# 268	40:10	# 137—st.2		# 353
32:18	# 198—st.4	40:11	# 99—st.1	42:4	# 91
	# 241		# 137		# 257

ISAIAH

	# 351		# 349		# 55—st.2
53	# 6	**55:1**	# 26		# 137
	# 7		# 143—st.2	**59:7**	# 214—st.2
	# 30		# 322—st.2	**59:9**	# 184—st.4
	# 75		# 376		# 347
	# 116	**55:3**	# 337	**59:16**	# 185
	# 152—st.4	**55:4**	# 15	**60:1**	# 43—st.3
	# 251		# 330		# 56
	# 269—st.2	**55:6-7**	# 237		# 102
	# 332—st.4	**55:7**	# 57		# 210
53:2	# 31—st.3		# 74		# 248—st.2
53:3	# 6		# 147		# 296—st.1
	# 207—st.3		# 286—st.3	**60:1-3**	# 79—st.3
	# 357—st.4		# 293		# 323
53:3-4	# 312—st.2	**55:9**	# 209		# 342
53:3-6	# 217	**55:10**	# 352		# 347
	# 289—st.2	**56:1**	# 107—st.3		# 348
53:3-12	# 217	**56:2**	# 236—st.3	**60:3**	# 91
53:4	# 196	**56:6-7**	# 33—st.3		# 357
	# 244—st.4		# 236—st.3	**60:10**	# 107—st.2
53:4-6	# 65	**56:7**	# 100	**60:14**	# 356
	# 152—st.4	**57:2**	# 4	**60:16**	# 353
53:4-12	# 154		# 141—st.4	**60:19**	# 43—st.3
	# 361		# 284		# 101
53:5	# 24	**57:13**	# 130		# 102
53:5-6	# 147	**57:15**	# 26		# 119
53:6	# 64—st.3		# 82		# 190
	# 155—st.2		# 132		# 248—st.2
	# 322—st.3		# 159		# 257
53:7	# 364		# 237	**60:19-20**	# 72
53:9	# 31—st.3		# 279		# 210
53:10	# 2	**57:18**	# 125	**60:20**	# 25
	# 24	**57:19**	# 268		# 222—st.3
53:12	# 65	**57:20**	# 181		# 259
54:7-8	# 365	**58:8**	# 101		# 305
54:7-10	# 33		# 294	**61:1**	# 257
	# 39	**58:9**	# 360		# 266
	# 101	**58:11**	# 109		# 278
	# 337		# 125		# 357
54:8	# 74		# 158		# 378
54:10	# 203		# 162	**61:1-4**	# 65
	# 329—st.3		# 198	**61:2-3**	# 63
	# 365		# 306	**61:3**	# 90—st.2
54:11	# 69—st.1	**58:13-14**	# 236	**61:10**	# 89
54:14	# 102	**59:1**	# 43—st.3		# 107

JEREMIAH

31:9-11	# 286	42:3	# 198		
31:12	# 169	42:6	# 265—st.2	**EZEKIEL**	
	# 259	46:27	# 109	3:19	# 257—st.2
	# 356	50:5	# 301	8:17	# 82
31:34	# 178—st.4		# 329—st.3	9:9	# 82
31:35	# 8	50:6	# 38—st.2	11:19	# 239
	# 271		# 64—st.3		# 279
	# 353		# 322—st.3		# 327
32:17-20	# 8	50:17	# 38—st.2		# 374
	# 39	50:38	# 237	16:60	# 114
	# 101	51:5	# 107—st.2	16:62	# 114
	# 103	51:15	# 8	18:4	# 63
	# 105	51:17	# 237		# 107
	# 190			18:23	# 257—st.2
	# 273			18:31	# 239
	# 331	**LAMENTATIONS**			# 293
32:18	# 89	2:15	# 169	18:32	# 257—st.2
	# 138		# 170	20:12	# 236
32:19	# 113—st.2	3:21-26	# 33		# 283
32:39-40	# 299—st.2		# 107		# 339
	# 353—st.2		# 114	33:11	# 270
32:40	# 114		# 329	34	# 115
32:42	# 301		# 337		# 125
33:6	# 102—st.2	3:22	# 74		# 325
33:8	# 147		# 113	34:6	# 38
	# 178—st.4		# 286—st.3	34:12	# 139—st.4
	# 217—st.2	3:22-23	# 4—st.2	34:12-16	# 269—st.1
	# 293		# 365		# 289
	# 361	3:22-25	# 203	34:13-15	# 322—st.2
33:9	# 200	3:23	# 32	34:14	# 99
33:11	# 13	3:24-26	# 241		# 170—st.2
	# 190	3:27	# 88—st.3	34:14-15	# 286—st.1
	# 203	3:31-32	# 107	34:14-23	# 286
	# 256		# 337	34:15-16	# 155—
	# 270	3:32	# 365		st.2 & 3
	# 292	3:41	# 87—st.4	34:16	# 322—st.3
	# 322	5:19	# 63	34:23	# 269—st.1
	# 337		# 82		# 286
	# 365		# 114		# 289
33:14	# 301		# 241—st.3		# 322
33:15-16	# 117		# 256	34:25	# 268
	# 234		# 270	36:22	# 132
33:20	# 316		# 316—last st.	36:25	# 23
35:15	# 293		# 318		# 57
36:2	# 45—st.2 & 3	5:21	# 327		# 111
					# 147

	# 180	**3:28**	# 369		# 316—last st.
	# 193	**4:3**	# 3		# 326—st.3
	# 229		# 63	**9:4**	# 114
	# 286—st.3		# 256	**9:5**	# 38—st.2
	# 335		# 270	**9:7-17**	# 107
	# 374	**4:34**	# 318	**9:9**	# 178—st.4
36:25-27	# 108	**4:34-37**	# 103	**9:18**	# 337
36:26	# 239		# 107	**9:24**	# 65
	# 279		# 256	**10:12**	# 349
	# 379		# 270	**10:18-19**	# 180—st.1
36:26-27	# 112	**4:37**	# 151	**12:2**	# 215—st.4
36:27	# 43—st.2		# 326		# 285—st.4
	# 48	**5:4**	# 237	**12:3**	# 257
	# 61	**5:23**	# 237		# 278
	# 133	**6:10**	# 68		# 357
	# 265		# 230		# 378
	# 297		# 274	**12:10**	# 23
	# 298		# 307		# 57—st.3
37:9-10	# 48		# 352		# 185
37:14	# 48		# 360		# 193
	# 61	**6:23**	# 81		# 335
	# 297		# 86		# 374
	# 298	**6:26**	# 114		
37:24-25	# 339—st.3		# 256	**HOSEA**	
	# 373—st.3		# 318	**1:9-10**	# 185—st.4
39:7	# 131	**7:9**	# 38—st.1	**1:10**	# 39
	# 132		# 63	**2:15**	# 277
39:29	# 61		# 107	**2:18**	# 211
	# 133		# 159	**2:19**	# 365
	# 297		# 256	**2:19-20**	# 33
43:26	# 308	**7:10**	# 313	**2:23**	# 39
46:1	# 267		# 326	**6:3**	# 117—st.3
DANIEL		**7:13**	# 63		# 320—st.2
			# 159	**10:12**	# 117—st.3
2:20	# 151		# 256	**11:1-8**	# 248
	# 292	**7:13-14**	# 65	**12:6**	# 37
2:20-23	# 37		# 107		# 101
	# 101		# 166—st.4		# 108
	# 103		# 206		# 125
	# 107		# 326	**13:14**	# 185—st.4
	#159	**7:14**	# 316—last st.		# 215—st.4
2:22	# 195	**7:22**	# 63		# 264—st.2
	# 210		# 107		# 312
2:23	# 68		# 159		# 313
	# 230		# 256	**14:2**	# 353
	# 352	**7:27**	# 191	**14:4**	# 64—st.3
2:35-44	# 254				

HOSEA

14:9	# 127
	# 198

JOEL

1—3	# 103
2:12	# 239
2:13	# 74
2:26	# 171
2:28-29	# 61
	# 297
3:10	# 56—st.2
3:13	# 121
3:16	# 241
	# 329

AMOS

2:11	# 257—st.4
4:4	# 350
4:5	# 68
	# 230
	# 352
4:13	# 271
5:23	# 62—st.2
5:24	# 91—st.4
7:8	# 122—st.2
8:11-13	# 47
	# 194
8:12	# 83

JONAH

1:4	# 181
1:6	# 209
2:9	# 68
	# 230
	# 272
	# 352
4:2	# 33
	# 104
	# 331
	# 337
	# 353

MICAH

3:8	# 297
	# 298
4:5	# 237
	# 347

4:7	# 316—last st.
5:4	# 151
	# 269—st.1
6:6	# 100
6:8	# 237
	# 239
7:7	# 286—st.2
7:8	# 102
	# 128
	# 162—st.3
	# 192—st.3
	# 210
	# 305
	# 323
	# 342
	# 347
7:18	# 24—st.5
	# 64
	# 178—st.4
	# 244—st.2
	# 293
7:18-19	# 19
	# 74
7:18-20	# 39
	# 101
	# 114
	# 337
	# 365

NAHUM

1:3	# 90
	# 107
	# 353
	# 378
1:7	# 99
	# 158
	# 175
	# 178
	# 241
	# 322
1:7-8	# 3
	# 103
	# 107

HABAKKUK

1:12	# 103

	# 132
	# 159
2:2	# 45—st.3
2:18	# 237
2:20	# 73
	# 100
	# 200
3:2	# 279
	# 327
3:4	# 210
3:17-18	# 272
	# 296—st.4
3:18	# 269—st.2
3:18-19	# 3
	# 190
3:19	# 102
	# 158

ZEPHANIAH

1:17	# 227—st.2
2:11	# 91
3:5	# 107
	# 159—st.2
3:17	# 101
	# 286—st.4

HAGGAI

2:4	# 247—st.4
2:5	# 114
	# 298
2:7	# 20
2:8	# 350
2:8-9	# 16

ZECHARIAH

2:5	# 210
	# 378—st.2
2:10	# 99
	# 218
2:13	# 200
4:6	# 298
8:13	# 216
8:16	# 265—st.3
9:9	# 10
	# 280
	# 339—st.3 & 4
9:15	# 286—st.2

9:29	# 238		# 355—st.4	**11:29**	# 131—st.4
9:35	# 342—st.2		# 371		# 147—st.4
9:36	# 38—st.2	**10:38-39**	# 88	**12:1-13**	# 236
	# 125		# 121		# 283
	# 135		# 205		# 339
	# 214		# 245	**12:6**	# 303
	# 269—st.1		# 249	**12:8**	# 315
	# 370		# 311		# 358
9:36-38	# 278		# 372	**12:13**	# 342—st.2
9:37-38	# 68	**10:42**	# 1	**12:20**	# 154—st.3
	# 69		# 88	**12:20-21**	# 3
	# 121		# 121		# 320
9:38	# 91		# 245		# 338—st.3
	# 257		# 370	**12:21**	# 139
	# 357	**11:3**	# 117		# 179
	# 378	**11:5**	# 193—st.4		# 183
10:6	# 38—st.2	**11:15**	# 265—st.2		# 240—st.2 & 3
10:16	# 261	**11:19**	# 139—st.2		# 244
	# 286		# 157		# 309
	# 351		# 175		# 319
10:20	# 76		# 187		# 380—st.1
	# 265—st.3		# 228	**12:22-23**	# 342—st.2
10:21	# 175—st.3		# 360	**12:23**	# 117
10:22	# 18—st.1	**11:25-26**	# 103	**12:34**	# 212
	# 97—st.2	**11:25-27**	# 159		# 265—st.3
10:28	# 175—st.3	**11:28**	# 139—st.2	**12:36**	# 1—st.3
10:29-31	# 338		# 147—st.3	**12:40**	# 332—st.3
10:32	# 357		# 150	**12:50**	# 76
	# 376		# 176		# 82
10:33	# 165—st.1		# 198—st.4		# 141—st.2
	# 171		# 240—st.3		# 223
10:37	# 220		# 263		# 281
	# 224		# 266		# 286—st.4
10:37-38	# 172		# 293	**13:9**	# 265—st.2
	# 293		# 376	**13:16**	# 265
10:38	# 1	**11:28-29**	# 57—st.2	**13:24-30**	# 68
	# 40	**11:28-30**	# 25		# 69
	# 98		# 69—st.2	**13:31**	# 255
	# 174		# 71	**13:36-38**	# 54
	# 175—st.3		# 143—st.1	**13:36-43**	# 68
	# 196—st.4		# 214—st.2		# 69
	# 221		# 218	**13:38**	# 91
	# 248—st.4		# 226	**13:43**	# 128
	# 278		# 246		# 217—st.4
	# 330—st.1		# 324—st.1		# 265—st.2

	# 313		# 330—st.1	**18:21-35**	# 337
	# 357—refrain	**16:24-25**	# 121	**18:23**	# 1—st.3
14:7	# 301		# 174	**18:33**	# 319
14:13-21	# 47		# 205	**19:2**	# 342—st.2
14:14	# 135		# 245	**19:4-6**	# 118
	# 319		# 249		# 243
14:22-32	# 181		# 371		# 250
14:27	# 175	**16:24-26**	# 98	**19:16**	# 320—st.3
	# 178—st.3		# 355—st.4	**19:17**	# 322
14:30-32	# 36—st.2	**16:24-27**	# 221	**19:21**	# 37—st.3
14:31	# 15		# 311		# 175—st.3
14:33	# 303	**16:26**	# 165—st.2		# 350—st.4
	# 367	**16:27**	# 78—st.2		# 370
14:36	# 342—st.2		# 166	**19:26**	# 107
	# 374		# 262—st.5		# 303
15:18	# 239	**16:27-28**	# 119—st.4	**19:27-28**	# 88
15:22	# 339		# 168		# 221
15:24	# 38—st.2		# 206		# 249
	# 286	**16:28**	# 355	**19:28**	# 380
15:25	# 367	**17:2**	# 128	**19:29**	# 214—st.2
15:28	# 238		# 210		# 355—st.4
	# 374		# 304	**20:16**	# 176
15:30	# 342—st.2		# 305	**20:17-19**	# 262
15:32	# 135		# 323	**20:19**	# 207—st.3
16:15-18	# 50	**17:12**	# 196		# 332
	# 55		# 251	**20:22**	# 22
	# 148	**17:18**	# 342—st.2		# 196—st.4
	# 188	**17:20**	# 80		# 371
	# 254		# 346	**20:22-23**	# 221
	# 314	**18:11**	# 269—st.2		# 330—st.1
16:16	# 50	**18:11-14**	# 38—st.2	**20:26-28**	# 1—st.1
16:18	# 50		# 155—st.2		# 97
	# 96—st.1		# 322—st.3		# 121
	# 254	**18:12**	# 286—st.2		# 249
	# 264	**18:14**	# 51		# 311
	# 316		# 257—st.1	**20:28**	# 65
16:19	# 276—st.3	**18:17**	# 152—st.4		# 120—st.3
16:21	# 116	**18:19**	# 54		# 163
16:24	# 22	**18:20**	# 31		# 215—st.3 & 4
	# 40		# 44		# 217
	# 172		# 50—st.2 & 3		# 262
	# 175—st.3		# 139		# 185—st.4
	# 196—st.4		# 152—st.1		# 345
	# 248—st.4		# 161		# 361
	# 288		# 309	**20:30**	# 339—st.3

MATTHEW

26:32	# 126		# 98—st.4		# 319
26:34	# 171	**28:1-8**	# 196—st.3		# 324
26:36-45	# 343		# 312—st.3		# 380—st.2
26:36-56	# 371—st.2	**28:1-9**	# 53		
26:36-68	# 196		# 58	**MARK**	
26:38-39	# 251		# 173		
26:39	# 22		# 252	**1:1-3**	# 65
	# 196—st.4		# 315	**1:10**	# 48
	# 223		# 358		# 62
26:41	# 225—st.2	**28:1-10**	# 98—st.4		# 297
	# 295—st.2		# 262—st.4		# 342—st.3
	# 360	**28:5-6**	# 332	**1:11**	# 79—st.1
26:42	# 196—st.4	**28:6**	# 126	**1:12-13**	# 312—st.2
	# 223		# 144	**1:16-20**	# 73
26:46-75	# 98—st.2	**28:6-7**	# 339—st.2		# 245
26:57-68	# 371—st.3	**28:9**	# 367		# 355—st.4
26:63	# 79—st.1	**28:18**	# 11	**1:32-34**	# 319—st.1
26:63-64	# 276		# 53—st.2 & 3	**1:35**	# 274
26:64	# 144		# 70		# 307
	# 145		# 173		# 360
	# 168		# 182	**1:37**	# 374—st.4
	# 182		# 215—st.2	**1:39-45**	# 319
	# 363—st.1		# 269—st.3	**1:40-42**	# 178—st.3
26:69-75	# 165		# 276—st.3	**1:41**	# 135
	# 171		# 320	**2:5**	# 147
27:1-30	# 98—st.2	**28:19**	# 8—st.4		# 319—st.2
27:1-66	# 196		# 63	**2:5-12**	# 178—st.3
	# 312—st.3		# 91	**2:9**	# 283—st.2
27:11-26	# 371—st.3		# 97—st.4	**2:9-11**	# 155—st.3
27:24	# 251		# 131—st.4	**2:9-12**	# 240—st.4
	# 333		# 132		# 319
27:24-50	# 6		# 257	**2:14**	# 73
	# 7		# 278		# 355—st.4
	# 30		# 351		# 371
27:26-54	# 262—st.2		# 378		# 372
27:27-60	# 359	**28:19-20**	# 54	**2:17**	# 183—st.3
27:28-50	# 116		# 212	**2:27-28**	# 236
	# 151—st.4		# 357		# 283
	# 269—st.2	**28:20**	# 4		# 339
27:29	# 320—st.1		# 36	**3:1-5**	# 178—st.3
27:29-31	# 207—st.3		# 126	**3:10**	# 178—st.3
27:33	# 328		# 184—st.4	**3:11**	# 79—st.1
27:41	# 207—st.3		# 218		# 367
27:57-60	# 196—st.2		# 228	**3:35**	# 223
27:57-66	# 53—st.1&2		# 262		# 281

MARK

	# 156		# 269—st.3		# 97
	# 192		# 276—st.2		# 257
	# 205		# 363		# 351
13:10	# 54	**14:66-72**	# 165		# 357
	# 81		# 171		# 378
	# 91	**15:1-9**	# 98—st.2	**16:15-16**	# 278
	# 257	**15:1-15**	# 371—st.3	**16:16**	# 19
	# 278	**15:1-39**	# 6		# 57
	# 327	**15:1-47**	# 196		# 146—st.2
	# 351		# 312—st.3		# 180
	# 357	**15:15-39**	# 262—st.2		# 184—st.3
	# 378	**15:16-17**	# 251		# 263
13:11	# 61	**15:16-19**	# 207—st.3	**16:19**	# 262—st.4
	# 265—st.3		# 320		
13:26-27	# 326	**15:16-47**	# 359		
	# 363—st.1	**15:20-41**	# 98—st.3		
13:26-37	# 168	**15:22**	# 196		
	# 206		# 328		
13:31	# 145—st.2	**15:25**	# 359		
13:32-36	# 146—st.4	**15:25-28**	# 312—st.3		
13:32-37	# 363	**15:40-47**	# 262—st.3		
14:22-26	# 5	**15:42-46**	# 196—st.2		
	# 46	**15:42-47**	# 98—st.4		
	# 129	**15:46**	# 312—st.3		
	# 202	**15:46-47**	# 53—st.1&2		
14:24	# 23	**16:1-6**	# 53		
	# 116—st.2		# 58		
	# 217—st.2		# 98—st.4		
	# 229		# 173		
	# 244—st.2		# 252		
	# 263—st.2		# 262—st.4		
	# 269—st.2		# 312—st.3		
	# 335		# 332		
14:26	# 343	**16:1-8**	# 196—st.3		
14:26-41	# 98—st.1	**16:1-14**	# 173		
14:32-41	# 343		# 252		
14:32-50	# 371—st.2	**16:6**	# 126		
14:36	# 223		# 144		
14:42-72	# 98—st.2	**16:9**	# 236		
14:53-65	# 371—st.3		# 283		
14:62	# 144		# 339		
	# 145		# 351—st.1		
	# 168		# 358		
	# 206	**16:15**	# 54		
	# 207		# 91		

LUKE

1:1-3	# 65
1:10	# 274
1:14	# 12
1:26-38	# 65
	# 94
	# 120—st.2
	# 247—st.2
1:31-33	# 117
1:32	# 79—st.1
	# 170—st.3
1:32-33	# 70
	# 182
	# 206—st.4
	# 234
	# 276
	# 380
1:33	# 258
	# 316—last st.
	# 317
	# 336—refrain
1:35	# 8—st.3
	# 63
	# 77
	# 79—st.1
1:37	# 303
1:46-55	# 336
1:46-75	# 49
	# 189
	# 299

1:47	# 183	**2:1-7**	# 35	**3:6**	# 140
	# 184		# 65		# 351
	# 276		# 233	**3:16**	# 61
1:50	# 74		# 247		# 297
	# 286		# 341	**3:22**	# 8—st.4
	# 365	**2:1-20**	# 258		# 62
1:54-55	# 105	**2:4-7**	# 260		# 297
	# 373—st.3	**2:6-20**	# 362		# 353
1:68-69	# 41	**2:7**	# 355—st.1	**3:23-38**	# 373—st.3
	# 89	**2:7-20**	# 12	**4:1-14**	# 312—st.2
	# 189		# 20	**4:4**	# 310—st.1
	# 233		# 21	**4:16**	# 236
	# 317		# 94		# 283
	# 336		# 166		# 339
	# 353		# 290	**4:18**	# 266
1:68-73	# 65		# 317	**4:22**	# 146
	# 114		# 336	**4:32**	# 212
1:69	# 373—st.3		# 373		# 319—st.1
1:71	# 211	**2:10-11**	# 120		# 344—st.1
1:74-75	# 310		# 189	**4:41**	# 79—st.1
1:75	# 239	**2:10-14**	# 92	**5:3**	# 287
1:77	# 140	**2:10-20**	# 110	**5:8**	# 178—st.3
	# 142—st.4	**2:11**	# 247	**5:10-11**	# 73
1:77-79	# 59	**2:11-12**	# 260	**5:11**	# 9
	# 110	**2:12**	# 35		# 22
	# 120	**2:13-14**	# 120		# 153
	# 200		# 233		# 174
	# 290		# 262—st.1		# 205
	# 304		# 312—st.1	**5:17**	# 155—st.3
	# 323		# 355—st.1		# 178—st.3
	# 355—st.2	**2:14**	# 21		# 319—st.1
1:78	# 101	**2:15**	# 233	**5:20-24**	# 240—st.4
	# 337	**2:16**	# 35	**5:24**	# 155—st.3
1:78-79	# 56	**2:29**	# 284	**5:27**	# 355—st.4
	# 67	**2:29-32**	# 323	**5:27-28**	# 371
	# 234—st.3		# 336		# 372
1:79	# 70—st.3	**2:30**	# 265—st.1	**5:28**	# 153
	# 102	**2:32**	# 59	**6:1-10**	# 236
	# 125		# 159		# 283
	# 198—st.1		# 234—st.3		# 339
	# 268	**2:40**	# 260	**6:12**	# 274
	# 284—st.3	**2:52**	# 260		# 307
	# 305		# 355		# 360
	# 342	**3:5**	# 78—st.3	**6:13**	# 73
	# 347		# 124—st.4	**6:18**	# 193—st.4

LUKE

20:17	# 50	**22:39-54**	# 196			# 312—st.3
	# 55		# 371—st.3	**24:1-12**	# 98—st.4
	# 314	**22:41-44**	# 152—st.2		# 252
20:17-18	# 254	**22:42**	# 223	**24:1-48**	# 173
20:21	# 212	**22:43**	# 152—st.3	**24:5-7**	# 339
20:36	# 51	**22:47-71**	# 98—st.2	**24:6**	# 126
	# 52	**22:51**	# 319—st.1		# 144
	# 169	**22:56-62**	# 165		# 173
	# 208		# 171		# 252
	# 313	**22:63-65**	# 207—st.3	**24:8**	# 212
	# 368	**22:66-71**	# 371—st.3		# 344—st.1
20:36-38	# 86	**22:69**	# 182	**24:19**	# 139—st.4
20:38	# 218		# 215—st.1	**24:26**	# 116
21:15	# 102		# 217—st.3		# 196
21:19	# 221—st.3		# 276—st.2		# 217—st.2 & 3
	# 249—st.3	**22:70**	# 79—st.1		# 251
	# 310	**23**	# 312—st.3		# 289
21:22	# 326	**23:1-25**	# 98—st.2	**24:26-27**	# 312
21:25-36	# 363—st.3		# 371—st.3	**24:27**	# 45
21:27	# 124—st.5	**23:1-46**	# 6		# 47
	# 262—st.5	**23:1-56**	# 196		# 194
21:27-28	# 168	**23:6**	# 116—st.1		# 255
	# 206	**23:11**	# 207—st.3	**24:29**	# 4
21:28	# 204	**23:24-47**	# 262—st.2		# 14
21:31	# 206	**23:26-49**	# 98		# 72
21:33	# 145—st.2	**23:26-53**	# 359		# 304
	# 310—st.3	**23:32-33**	# 328		# 367
	# 317—st.1	**23:34**	# 319—st.2	**24:30**	# 5
21:36	# 98—st.1	**23:36**	# 207—st.3		# 46
22:4	# 251	**23:38**	# 182		# 129
22:14-20	# 5	**23:42**	# 5—st.4		# 202
	# 46	**23:42-43**	# 209	**24:32**	# 47—st.3 & 4
	# 129	**23:43**	# 57—st.4		# 83
	# 202		# 58—st.3		# 194
22:20	# 217—st.2	**23:48-56**	# 262—st.3		# 255
	# 229	**23:50**	# 196—st.2		# 377
	# 244—st.2	**23:50-56**	# 53—st.1 & 2	**24:34**	# 53
	# 269—st.2				# 58
	# 328	**23:53**	# 312—st.3		# 126
	# 366—st.2	**23:54-56**	# 262—st.3		# 144
22:29-44	# 343	**24:1-7**	# 53		# 332
22:31-32	# 165		# 58	**24:39**	# 126
22:37	# 6		# 262—st.4	**24:45**	# 47—st.3 & 4
	# 116		# 332		# 194
22:39-46	# 98	**24:1-9**	# 196—st.3		# 255

24:46	# 116		# 133—st.1		# 345
	# 173		# 143—st.3	**1:16-17**	# 19
	# 262		# 184—st.4		# 57
	# 312		# 200		# 74
24:46-48	# 29		# 222—st.3		# 111
24:47	# 54		# 244—st.3		# 146
	# 91		# 248—st.2		# 180
	# 183—st.3	**1:4-9**	# 101	**1:17**	# 326—st.2
	# 257		# 257		# 329
	# 278		# 323		# 340—st.2
	# 309		# 355—st.2		# 355—st.2
	# 351	**1:5**	# 67		# 371—st.4
	# 357		# 155—st.4	**1:18**	# 159
24:49	# 112		# 195		# 303—st.1
	# 133—st.3	**1:9**	# 20—st.2	**1:29**	# 116—st.2
	# 134—st.2		# 56		# 117
	# 297		# 247		# 147
	# 301		# 305		# 222
24:50-53	# 262—st.4		# 342		# 319—st.3
24:52	# 184		# 347		# 333—st.3
	# 367	**1:12**	# 2		# 357—st.4
24:53	# 87—st.4		# 37—st.2		# 364
			# 51	**1:32**	# 62
JOHN			# 52		# 342—st.3
			# 178	**1:32-33**	# 297
1:1	# 133—st.1		# 187	**1:33**	# 61
	# 233—st.3		# 263	**1:34**	# 79—st.1
	# 258		# 275		# 303
	# 289—st.2		# 309	**1:36**	# 319—st.3
1:1-3	# 31		# 324—st.2		# 333—st.3
1:1-5	# 255		# 344	**1:43**	# 355—st.4
1:1-14	# 59	**1:12-13**	# 24—st.4 & 5	**1:51**	# 227—st.3
	# 159	**1:13**	# 379	**2:22**	# 146—st.2
	# 273	**1:14**	# 45—st.3		# 255
1:3	# 17		# 63—st.2	**2:23**	# 179
	# 87		# 83		# 309
1:4	# 28—st.3		# 120	**3:1-8**	# 379
	# 70—st.2		# 155—st.1	**3:1-15**	# 132
	# 305		# 200	**3:2**	# 355—st.3
	# 340—st.3		# 233—st.3	**3:3**	# 214—st.4
	# 342		# 255		# 319—st.2
	# 344—st.3		# 258		# 379
	# 347		# 262	**3:3-17**	# 120—st.3
1:4-5	# 56		# 340—st.2	**3:5-6**	# 61
	# 128		# 342	**3:5-7**	# 48

JOHN

3:6	# 108—st.1	**3:36**	# 184—st.3		# 240
3:7	# 379		# 263		# 269
3:8	# 159		# 278		# 367
3:11	# 28		# 344		# 380
	# 212	**4:10**	# 26	**5:24**	# 194
	# 257		# 135—st.2		# 263
	# 278		# 143—st.2		# 340
	# 351		# 228—st.5		# 344
3:13-17	# 33		# 322—st.2		# 377
	# 125	**4:10-14**	# 96—st.2		# 379
	# 247—st.3	**4:13-14**	# 143—st.2	**5:27**	# 326
	# 262		# 376	**5:30**	# 82
	# 319—st.2	**4:14**	# 15—st.2		# 122
	# 345		# 26		# 153
3:15	# 278—st.2		# 115		# 223
3:15-17	# 215—st.3&4	**4:23**	# 43	**5:31**	# 207—st.3
	# 257	**4:24**	# 100	**5:35**	# 128
	# 376	**4:34**	# 88		# 162—st.3
3:16	# 146		# 97—st.1		# 210
	# 152		# 216		# 342
	# 154		# 223	**5:37**	# 159
	# 160		# 312—st.2		# 303—st.1
	# 244—st.2	**4:35**	# 68	**5:39**	# 45
	# 263		# 69		# 47
	# 337	**4:35-38**	# 121		# 83
	# 357—st.3	**4:36**	# 320—st.3		# 107—st.3
	# 364	**4:42**	# 91		# 219—st.3
3:16-17	# 28		# 278		# 255
	# 70		# 351		# 377
	# 149		# 361	**5:39-40**	# 320—st.3
	# 214	**4:46-53**	# 319	**5:40**	# 176
3:18	# 3		# 342—st.2		# 266
3:19	# 342	**5:5-9**	# 178—st.3	**6:1-14**	# 47
	# 347		# 342—st.2	**6:2**	# 228—st.1
3:19-21	# 101	**5:6**	# 374		# 319—st.1
	# 195	**5:14**	# 374	**6:27**	# 70—st.2
	# 323	**5:17**	# 312—st.2	**6:29**	# 346
3:27	# 93	**5:18**	# 182	**6:32-35**	# 15—st.2
3:29	# 23—st.3		# 276		# 66—st.3
3:31	# 269—st.3	**5:19-29**	# 154		# 99—st.2
3:33	# 214	**5:20**	# 146	**6:35**	# 47
3:33-34	# 63	**5:22**	# 326		# 135—st.2
	# 132	**5:22-23**	# 11		# 139—st.2
3:34	# 276—st.2	**5:23**	# 42		# 143—st.2
3:35	# 276—st.3		# 79		# 184

6:35-58	# 5		# 223			# 369
	# 46		# 265	**8:32**	# 47—st.2 & 3	
	# 129	**7:37**	# 26			# 81
	# 202		# 57			# 192—st.4
6:37	# 193		# 176			# 198—st.2
	# 228—st.4		# 266			# 265
	# 266		# 376			# 266
	# 286—st.3	**7:37-38**	# 143—st.2			# 340—st.2
	# 324—st.3	**7:38**	# 263	**8:34-36**	# 42—st.3	
6:38-39	# 223		# 324—st.3			# 240—st.4
6:40	# 28—st.3	**7:39**	# 63	**8:35**		# 73
	# 67		# 132	**8:36**	# 28—st.2	
	# 253	**7:40**	# 139—st.4			# 154—st.1
	# 259	**7:42**	# 117			# 217
	# 263	**7:46**	# 215—st.2			# 244—st.2
6:41	# 91	**8:2**	# 287			# 286—st.3
	# 135—st.2	**8:11**	# 57	**8:46**		# 146
6:44-51	# 177		# 74	**8:51-56**	# 215—st.2	
6:45	# 212	**8:12**	# 56	**8:54**		# 79
6:47	# 28—st.3		# 59	**8:58**		# 258
	# 263		# 79—st.3			# 318
6:48-51	# 66—st.3		# 91—st.3			# 364
	# 99—st.2		# 101	**9:1-7**		# 342
	# 115		# 128	**9:4**		# 14
	# 135—st.2		# 133—st.1			# 25
6:51	# 15—st.2		# 143—st.3			# 32
	# 139—st.2		# 155—st.4			# 72
6:53-56	# 333		# 159			# 97—st.3
	# 335		# 162—st.3			# 106
6:56-58	# 37		# 175			# 208
6:58	# 15—st.2		# 184—st.4			# 312—st.2
	# 66—st.3		# 195			# 378—st.3
	# 99—st.2		# 228—st.3	**9:5**		# 59
6:63	# 48		# 244—st.3			# 195
	# 62		# 247			# 324
6:68	# 289—st.2		# 248—st.2	**9:38**		# 367
	# 320—st.3		# 305	**10:1-9**		# 246
	# 344		# 323	**10:1-16**	# 269—st.1	
	# 377		# 342			# 286
7:14	# 287		# 347			# 325
7:17	# 76	**8:21**	# 257—st.2	**10:1-18**	# 155—st.2	
	# 82	**8:29-30**	# 212			# 322
	# 141—st.2	**8:30**	# 344—st.1	**10:3**	# 99—st.1	
	# 212	**8:31**	# 18—st.4			# 293
	# 219—st.2		# 225	**10:3-5**		# 15

	# 347		# 244—st.4		# 214
13:1	# 157		# 325		# 297
	# 160		# 346		# 304
	# 186	**14:1-3**	# 15—st.3	**14:16-18**	# 66—st.2
	# 248		# 36—st.3	**14:17**	# 133—st.1
	# 286		# 222—st.4		# 134—st.4
	# 287	**14:1-6**	# 324		# 146—st.3
	# 364		# 328		# 198—st.2
13:3-17	# 311		# 355—st.2	**14:18**	# 15
13:4-17	# 97—st.1	**14:2**	# 228—st.5		# 71
13:7	# 103		# 291—st.4		# 155—st.4
13:13	# 56		# 306—st.3		# 178
	# 289—st.2	**14:2-3**	# 144—st.4		# 184
13:13-14	# 249		# 217—st.4		# 187
13:13-15	# 160— last st.		# 224—st.4		# 244—st.4
			# 368		# 269
13:13-17	# 37	**14:2-4**	# 58—st.3 & 4		# 324
13:14	# 287		# 253	**14:18-19**	# 175
13:15	# 147—st.4	**14:3**	# 138—st.4	**14:19**	# 28—st.3
	# 212		# 145		# 126
	# 288		# 168		# 142
	# 310—st.2		# 170		# 144
13:23	# 137—last st.		# 363		# 156
13:32-33	# 262	**14:6**	# 43—st.2		# 340—st.3
13:34	# 160		# 139—st.4	**14:20**	# 37
	# 287		# 198		# 267
13:34-35	# 37		# 246	**14:21**	# 214
	# 44		# 363—st.3	**14:23**	# 145—st.3
	# 87—st.3		# 274—last st.		# 224
	# 190		# 329		# 369
	# 299—st.4		# 340	**14:23-24**	# 43
	# 370	**14:12**	# 369		# 344
13:35	# 133—st.2	**14:13**	# 11—st.1	**14:24**	# 212
	# 109—st.4		# 31	**14:26**	# 43
	# 216		# 179		# 63
	# 249—st.2		# 244—st.1		# 112
14:1	# 66		# 309		# 146—st.3
	# 91		# 319		# 219—st.2
	# 139	**14:15**	# 287		# 265
	# 175	**14:15-18**	# 108—st.5		# 304—st.2
	# 178	**14:16**	# 61	**14:26-27**	# 66—st.2
	# 184		# 71	**14:27**	# 15
	# 187		# 134		# 24
	# 214	**14:16-17**	# 63—st.3		
	# 226		# 112		

	# 25	**15:10**	# 162		# 71
	# 70—st.3		# 369		# 304—st.2
	# 71	**15:10-11**	# 184	**16:7-14**	# 146—st.3
	# 73	**15:11**	# 15—st.2	**16:13**	# 43
	# 90		# 141—st.4		# 112
	# 95		# 178		# 133
	# 102		# 215—st.4		# 192—st.4
	# 124		# 220—st.2		# 198—st.2
	# 139		# 242		# 219—st.2
	# 150		# 248—st.3		# 310—st.4
	# 167		# 305		# 340—st.2
	# 198—st.1		# 320—st.2	**16:13-14**	# 265
	# 211	**15:12**	# 87—st.3	**16:13-15**	# 63
	# 226		# 232		# 132
	# 268	**15:13**	# 60—st.2		# 304
	# 284		# 70—st.4	**16:19-22**	# 320
	# 344—st.3		# 152		# 363
14:28	# 60		# 160	**16:20**	# 95
	# 168		# 186		# 220—st.3
	# 363		# 244—st.2		# 222—st.3
15:1-15	# 37		# 287		# 305
	# 108—st.4		# 364	**16:22**	# 126—st.3
	# 366—st.4	**15:13-15**	# 157		# 144
15:3	# 191		# 228		# 305
	# 321—st.4	**15:13-16**	# 360	**16:24**	# 215—st.4
15:4	# 4	**15:14**	# 245		# 274
	# 187—st.5		# 370		# 360
	# 205	**15:14-15**	# 36—st.1	**16:26**	# 179
	# 369		# 175		# 309
15:4-5	# 153		# 324	**16:33**	# 15
15:4-7	# 310—st.1	**15:15**	# 144—st.3		# 70—st.3
15:4-8	# 216	**15:16**	# 309		# 73
	# 311	**15:17-19**	# 249		# 102
15:8	# 1	**15:18-20**	# 97—st.2		# 124
15:9	# 157	**15:20**	# 245		# 125
	# 183—st.4	**15:26**	# 63—st.3		# 135
	# 219		# 112		# 150
	# 244		# 132		# 152—st.4
	# 303		# 133—st.1		# 164
15:9-10	# 160		# 146—st.3		# 165
	# 186		# 304—st.2		# 183
	# 287	**15:27**	# 39		# 184
15:9-11	# 242	**16:7**	# 61		# 198—st.1
	# 248—st.3		# 63—st.3		# 211
	# 305		# 66—st.2		# 218

	# 255		# 351		# 380—st.2
	# 263		# 357	**2:36**	# 28
	# 278—st.2		# 378		# 207
	# 309	**1:9**	# 207—st.4		# 269
	# 329—st.1		# 262—st.4		# 320
	# 340—st.3	**1:9-11**	# 206	**2:38**	# 48
	# 344		# 363		# 61
	# 377	**1:11**	# 124—st.5		# 62
21:9	# 22		# 262—st.5		# 74—st.4
21:15	# 220	**1:14**	# 274		# 133
21:15-17	# 1		# 307		# 214
	# 172	**1:18**	# 149		# 283—st.2
	# 216	**2:1-4**	# 48		# 297
	# 224		# 61		# 298
	# 245		# 297		# 319—st.2
	# 281	**2:1-16**	# 326	**2:38-39**	# 301
	# 287	**2:4**	# 112	**2:42**	# 5
21:15-19	# 88	**2:21**	# 179		# 202
	# 372		# 266		# 254
21:17	# 220		# 376		# 314
21:19	# 371	**2:24**	# 126	**2:46-47**	# 5
21:22	# 281—st.2		# 144		# 13
			# 262—st.4		# 202
		2:24-32	# 53	**2:47**	# 148
ACTS			# 58		# 188
			# 67		# 254
1:1	# 355—st.3		# 215	**3:1**	# 274
1:2-5	# 63—st.3		# 315		# 307
	# 214—st.2	**2:25**	# 51—st.2		# 360
1:3	# 126		# 178	**3:2**	# 267
	# 144		# 349	**3:6**	# 178—st.3
	# 262—st.4	**2:27**	# 137—st.5	**3:15**	# 126
1:4-5	# 61		# 314		# 144
1:5	# 62	**2:28**	# 183	**3:16**	# 309
1:6	# 214—st.4	**2:30-33**	# 70	**3:18**	# 6
1:8	# 54	**2:32**	# 126		# 116
	# 61		# 144		# 217
	# 91		# 212		# 251
	# 112		# 262—st.4	**3:19**	# 26
	# 133		# 312—st.3		# 74—st.4
	# 207—st.3	**2:33**	# 8—st.4		# 242
	# 212		# 63—st.3		# 286—st.3
	# 257		# 214—st.2		# 293
	# 278		# 217—st.3	**3:20**	# 363
	# 297		# 301	**3:36**	# 238
	# 342—st.3				

4:9-10	# 374	**6:5-15**	# 330—st.2	**10:43**	# 57
4:10-12	# 139	**7:1-60**	# 330—st.2		# 139
	# 244	**7:5**	# 301		# 146
4:11	# 50	**7:17**	# 301		# 179
	# 139—st.3	**7:22**	# 303—last st.		# 180
4:12	# 31	**7:26**	# 44		# 240
	# 42		# 161		# 244
	# 124		# 232		# 263
	# 139	**7:48**	# 50—st.2		# 278—st.2
	# 149		# 63		# 309
	# 176	**7:48-49**	# 302		# 319
	# 179	**7:50**	# 151		# 344
	# 183—st.2	**7:51**	# 62		# 376
	# 215		# 298	**11:14**	# 301—st.2
	# 244	**7:55**	# 104	**11:16**	# 61
	# 282	**8:1-4**	# 254		# 297
	# 309	**8:15**	# 48	**11:21**	# 263
	# 319		# 133	**12:2**	# 330
	# 329—st.1		# 297	**13:23**	# 301
	# 334—st.4	**8:32-33**	# 116		# 373—st.3
	# 351		# 217	**13:30**	# 312—st.3
4:24	# 138	**8:34**	# 326	**13:32**	# 257
	# 151	**8:37**	# 79—st.1		# 301
	# 292	**9:3**	# 159		# 351
	# 338	**9:3-5**	# 59	**13:32-33**	# 65
4:30	# 179	**9:16**	# 205	**13:33**	# 79—st.1
	# 309	**9:20**	# 79—st.1	**13:39**	# 238
4:31	# 112	**9:31**	# 63—st.3		# 263
	# 133		# 297		# 344
	# 297	**9:34**	# 122—st.3	**13:47**	# 342
4:32	# 56		# 178—st.3	**13:48**	# 320—st.3
	# 188		# 228—st.1	**13:52**	# 134—st.3
5:21	# 32		# 319	**14:9**	# 238
5:29	# 1—st.2	**10:9**	# 360	**14:10**	# 326
	# 88	**10:34**	# 376	**14:15**	# 8
5:30	# 81	**10:36**	# 211		# 82
	# 86		# 268		# 151
5:30-31	# 215	**10:38**	# 63—st.3	**14:17**	# 64
	# 217—st.3		# 117	**14:22**	# 165
	# 320		# 232—st.3		# 349
5:31	# 56—st.3		# 319—st.1	**14:27**	# 91
	# 269—st.3	**10:38-41**	# 312		# 135
	# 289—st.3	**10:40-41**	# 126		# 246
	# 380—st.2		# 144	**15:8**	# 48
5:32	# 61	**10:42**	# 326		# 63—st.3

	# 133		# 141	**20:35**	# 18—st.2 & 3
15:11	# 19		# 226		# 310—st.1
	# 57		# 227	**21:13**	# 330
	# 111		# 241	**21:14**	# 76
	# 139—st.3		# 292—st.3		# 82
	# 178—st.4	**17:27-28**	# 150		# 122
	# 180	**17:27-30**	# 237		# 223
	# 222—st.1	**17:28**	# 210		# 265
16:9-10	# 91		# 257—st.3	**22:15**	# 312
	# 278	**17:30**	# 74—st.4	**22:16**	# 57
16:10	# 257		# 278—st.2		# 180
	# 351		# 327		# 374
	# 357	**17:31**	# 326	**25:19**	# 126
	# 378	**18:9**	# 149		# 144
16:25	# 154	**18:10**	# 102	**26:6**	# 301
16:30-31	# 242	**18:28**	# 47	**26:13**	# 79—st.3
	# 266		# 83	**26:13-15**	# 59
16:31	# 146		# 255		# 159
	# 263	**19:17**	# 79	**26:17-18**	# 56
	# 278—st.2		# 269		# 357
	# 344		# 380—st.1	**26:18**	# 86
17:3	# 28	**20:7**	# 5		# 101
	# 116		# 46		# 195
	# 217		# 202		# 253
	# 262		# 208		# 278
	# 312—st.3		# 236		# 347
17:11	# 83	**20:21**	# 28	**26:20**	# 327
	# 194	**20:24**	# 19	**26:22**	# 113
	# 255—st.2 & 4		# 57	**26:23**	# 144
	# 377		# 163		# 312
17:24	# 38		# 216		
	# 50—st.2	**20:28**	# 148	**ROMANS**	
	# 151		# 281—st.3	**1:2**	# 45
	# 267		# 314		# 301
	# 331		# 333—st.3	**1:3**	# 117
17:24-26	# 56		# 345		# 363—st.3
	# 82	**20:32**	# 57	**1:3-4**	# 79—st.1
17:24-31	# 8		# 83		# 262
	# 17		# 86	**1:4**	# 53
	# 270		# 99		# 332
	# 302		# 169	**1:5**	# 88
17:27	# 4		# 194		# 97
	# 26		# 253	**1:6**	# 176
	# 76		# 368	**1:12**	# 44
	# 99		# 377		# 232

ROMANS

	# 305		# 332—st.2		# 352
	# 320—st.2		# 363—st.2		# 361
5:12-21	# 3—st.2	**6:11**	# 205	**8:1**	# 37
	# 361		# 218		# 347
5:15	# 135—st.2		# 340—st.3	**8:1-2**	# 42—st.3
	# 146		# 355—st.2		# 163
	# 371—st.4	**6:13**	# 9		# 240—st.4
5:18	# 24		# 22		# 266
	# 140		# 122		# 275
5:20	# 111		# 153		# 291
	# 189		# 192	**8:1-3**	# 154
	# 240—st.1		# 205	**8:1-4**	# 48
5:20-21	# 19		# 212		# 133
	# 139—st.3		# 215—st.4		# 298
	# 178—st.4		# 308	**8:3**	# 31—st.3
5:21	# 28—st.3		# 374—st.2	**8:6**	# 268
	# 70—st.2	**6:14**	# 19		# 303—last st.
	# 340—st.3		# 57—st.3	**8:7-8**	# 108—st.1
6:1-23	# 42—st.3		# 111	**8:8**	# 286—st.4
	# 240—st.4	**6:18**	# 156	**8:9**	# 62
6:2-11	# 28		# 205		# 112
	# 155—st.3		# 226		# 133
	# 244—st.2		# 286—st.3		# 297
6:2-18	# 154	**6:19**	# 9		# 298
6:3	# 218		# 192—st.4	**8:9-11**	# 48
6:4	# 41		# 212		# 134
	# 108		# 308	**8:11**	# 62
	# 144		# 310		# 112
	# 214—st.4		# 374—st.2	**8:11-15**	# 133
	# 347	**6:23**	# 28—st.3	**8:11-16**	# 61
	# 379		# 70—st.2	**8:14**	# 37—st.2
6:4-10	# 339		# 135—st.2		# 310—st.4
6:6	# 3		# 215—st.4	**8:14-17**	# 2
	# 338		# 269—st.2		# 24—st.4 & 5
6:8	# 156		# 320—st.3	**8:16**	# 51
	# 340—st.3	**7:2**	# 250		# 52
	# 355—st.2	**7:4**	# 55		# 146—st.3
6:9	# 126		# 188	**8:17**	# 253
	# 144		# 314		# 281—st.4
6:9-10	# 53	**7:18**	# 76	**8:21**	# 51
	# 58—st.2 & 3	**7:18-20**	# 178—st.3		# 52
	# 67	**7:18-25**	# 141—st.2	**8:23**	# 2
	# 173	**7:23**	# 193		# 24—st.4 & 5
	# 252	**7:25**	# 68		# 123
	# 276		# 230	**8:24**	# 135

8:24-25	# 26—st.4	**8:37**	# 80		# 351
	# 241		# 84		# 357
	# 329		# 197	**10:17**	# 137—st.1
8:26	# 63—st.3		# 264		# 255
	# 112		# 295		# 377
	# 274		# 300	**10:21**	# 74—st.2
	# 297		# 311		# 278—st.2
	# 298		# 375		# 293
	# 299—st.3	**8:37-39**	# 361—st.4	**11:2**	# 11—st.2
	# 307	**8:38-39**	# 157—st.3	**11:5-6**	# 19
	# 360		# 160		# 111
8:28	# 101	**9:1**	# 48	**11:6**	# 116—st.1
	# 103		# 133—st.1 & 4	**11:20**	# 238
	# 162		# 265—st.3	**11:22**	# 306
	# 167	**9:4**	# 301		# 322
8:29-30	# 11—st.2	**9:5**	# 81		# 365
	# 58		# 182	**11:29**	# 114
8:31	# 167		# 215—st.2	**11:33**	# 101
	# 349		# 269—st.3		# 103
8:32	# 15		# 276		# 107
	# 36	**9:8-9**	# 301		# 159
	# 123	**9:14**	# 103		# 361
	# 138—st.3		# 107	**11:36**	# 8
	# 203		# 159—st.2		# 292
8:32-39	# 71	**9:21**	# 122		# 345
8:34	# 24	**9:26**	# 51	**12:1**	# 84
	# 144		# 52		# 140—st.3
	# 217—st.3	**9:27**	# 185		# 157—st.2
	# 289—st.3	**10:3-4**	# 107—st.3		# 288
8:35	# 60—st.2	**10:4**	# 57		# 308
	# 157—st.3		# 180		# 355—st.4
	# 160		# 263		# 374
	# 183—st.4		# 329	**12:1-2**	# 9
8:35-39	# 33		# 344		# 122
	# 51—st.3	**10:8-9**	# 344		# 141
	# 119	**10:9**	# 263		# 153
	# 137—st.4	**10:10**	# 239		# 174
	# 152	**10:11-13**	# 376		# 192
	# 178	**10:12-15**	# 54		# 205
	# 186	**10:12-18**	# 91		# 212
	# 187	**10:13**	# 42	**12:2**	# 37
	# 248—st.1	**10:13-15**	# 378		# 76
	# 287	**10:14**	# 81—last st.		# 82
	# 324—st.3	**10:15**	# 257		# 125
	# 337		# 278		# 195

	# 223		# 347	**15:9-11**	# 182
	# 265	**13:14**	# 175	**15:13**	# 15
12:4-5	# 54—st.3	**14:6**	# 68		# 26—st.3
	# 188		# 230		# 41
	# 314	**14:7**	# 34—st.2		# 63—st.3
12:5	# 37		# 212		# 108—st.3
	# 44	**14:7-9**	# 218		# 167
	# 232		# 235		# 208—st.2
	# 264—st.3	**14:8**	# 155—st.5		# 241
12:6-8	# 93		# 187		# 329
12:9	# 104—st.2		# 322		# 344—st.3
	# 261	**14:8-9**	# 276	**15:15**	# 183—st.3
12:9-10	# 87—st.3	**14:9**	# 53	**15:19**	# 133—st.3
12:10	# 44		# 70	**15:32**	# 26
	# 108—st.4		# 215	**15:33**	# 4
	# 370		# 289		# 150
12:11	# 88		# 361		# 208
	# 97	**14:11**	# 63		# 226
	# 121		# 67		# 268
	# 141—st.2		# 256		# 284
	# 172		# 316—last st.	**16:17**	# 254
	# 245	**14:12**	# 1—st.3		# 314
	# 311	**14:17**	# 134—st.3	**16:20**	# 3
	# 355—st.4	**14:22-23**	# 80		# 208
	# 372		# 238		# 278—st.3
12:12	# 274	**15:1**	# 310—st.1		# 300
	# 307		# 370		# 338
	# 329	**15:1-7**	# 44		# 363—st.2
	# 360		# 232		# 375
12:18	# 82	**15:3**	# 174	**16:27**	# 159
12:21	# 104—st.2		# 248—st.3		# 345
	# 261	**15:4**	# 83		
13:1	# 82		# 135		
13:11	# 296—st.2		# 137—st.1	**1 CORINTHIANS**	
13:11-12	# 168		# 146—st.2	**1:2**	# 319
	# 326—st.1		# 213		# 334
	# 363—st.3		# 219		# 367
13:11-14	# 32		# 321	**1:4**	# 19
13:12	# 56	**15:5-6**	# 90—st.3		# 111
	# 97—st.3	**15:6**	# 345		# 146
	# 106	**15:8**	# 301		# 371—st.4
	# 295	**15:9**	# 11—st.3	**1:4-9**	# 114
	# 300—st.3		# 42	**1:5**	# 175
	# 327		# 240	**1:6**	# 149
	# 342		# 380	**1:7**	# 363

1:9	# 51—st.4	**1:31**	# 28		# 137	
	# 57		# 42		# 148	
	# 175		# 79		# 188	
	# 176		# 171		# 254	
	# 180		# 240		# 269	
	# 184		# 269		# 282	
	# 187		# 279		# 314	
	# 193	**2:2**	# 9—st.3	**3:16**	# 50—st.2 & 3	
	# 199		# 28		# 112	
	# 228		# 40		# 267	
1:10	# 44		# 140		# 297	
	# 56		# 164		# 298	
	# 161		# 219	**3:16-17**	# 63—st.3	
	# 232		# 279		# 214—st.3	
	# 314		# 320—st.2	**3:17**	# 310	
1:17-18	# 40		# 328	**4:1-2**	# 288	
1:17-19	# 29		# 366	**4:5**	# 326	
	# 164	**2:3**	# 102	**4:7**	# 93	
	# 177		# 291—st.3	**4:9**	# 34—st.2	
	# 328	**2:5**	# 80	**4:18**	# 56—st.3	
	# 366		# 238	**4:20**	# 151	
1:17-31	# 215	**2:7**	# 3	**5:2**	# 254—last st.	
	# 320	**2:9**	# 55—st.3	**5:7**	# 24	
1:18	# 135—last st.		# 170—st.1		# 140—st.2	
	# 140	**2:10**	# 43—st.2		# 251	
1:21	# 351		# 146—st.3		# 319—st.3	
1:23-25	# 29—st.1		# 265	**6:9**	# 261	
	# 101	**2:10-16**	# 61	**6:11**	# 48—st.2	
	# 164		# 133		# 57	
1:24	# 154—st.3		# 298		# 111	
	# 176	**2:11**	# 122—st.4		# 179	
	# 255—st.1	**2:13**	# 112		# 180	
	# 269		# 146—st.3		# 185	
1:27	# 180—st.1		# 219		# 193	
1:29	# 152—st.1		# 265—st.3		# 229	
1:30	# 123	**2:16**	# 303—last st.		# 309	
	# 242	**3:9**	# 1		# 335	
1:30-31	# 146		# 88		# 374	
	# 164		# 97	**6:13-20**	# 37	
	# 275		# 216	**6:15**	# 308	
	# 291		# 245	**6:17**	# 76	
	# 329	**3:10-11**	# 28—st.2		# 141	
	# 334	**3:11**	# 50		# 227	
	# 361		# 55	**6:19**	# 48	
	# 366		# 135		# 50—st.2 & 3	

1 CORINTHIANS

	# 61	**8:11**	# 310—st.1	**11:23-34**	# 129
	# 63—st.3	**9:10**	# 352	**11:25**	# 333
	# 112	**9:24**	# 34	**11:25-26**	# 244—st.2
	# 133		# 130	**11:26**	# 251
	# 218		# 368—st.4	**11:27-34**	# 202
	# 267	**9:24-27**	# 84	**12:2**	# 237
	# 298		# 330	**12:3**	# 133—st.4
6:19-20	# 153	**9:25-26**	# 197		# 146—st.3
	# 308		# 295		# 298
6:20	# 1—st.1		# 300	**12:4-11**	# 61
	# 22	**9:25-27**	# 18	**12:7**	# 133
	# 41		# 225		# 146—st.3
	# 122—st.4	**9:26**	# 264		# 297
	# 142		# 375	**12:9**	# 146—st.3
	# 156	**9:27**	# 192		# 238
	# 174	**10:1-4**	# 115	**12:12**	# 161
	# 192		# 282	**12:12-13**	# 314—st.2
	# 205	**10:4**	# 15—st.2	**12:12-14**	# 44
	# 269—st.2		# 50—st.1	**12:12-23**	# 264—st.3
	# 286—st.1		# 96	**12:12-27**	# 37
	# 345		# 187—st.2	**12:13**	# 56
	# 361—st.1	**10:6**	# 104—st.2		# 188
7:9	# 121		# 261	**12:26-27**	# 314—st.2
7:10-11	# 250	**10:11**	# 83	**12:27**	# 54—st.3
7:22	# 154—st.1	**10:12-13**	# 137—st.2		# 188
	# 240—st.4	**10:13**	# 130—st.3	**12:31**	# 198
	# 244—st.2		# 150—st.2	**13**	# 287
7:22-24	# 141		# 165	**13:4**	# 82
7:23	# 142		# 278—st.3	**13:6**	# 192—st.4
	# 156	**10:14**	# 237	**13:7**	# 18—st.4
	# 174	**10:16**	# 333	**13:12**	# 78
	# 205	**10:16-17**	# 37		# 119—st.3
	# 286—st.1	**10:16-22**	# 5		# 152—st.5
	# 361		# 129		# 169
7:23-24	# 155—st.3	**10:17**	# 44		# 183—st.1
7:31	# 4—st.2		# 161		# 212—st.4
8:5-6	# 210		# 264—st.3		# 253
8:6	# 8		# 314—st.2		# 259
	# 37	**10:26**	# 272		# 324—st.3
	# 56	**10:31**	# 345		# 368
	# 63	**11:3**	# 55	**14:15**	# 182—st.4
	# 73	**11:23-24**	# 45		# 240
	# 132	**11:23-25**	# 314—st.2		# 274
	# 159	**11:23-26**	# 202		# 307
	# 215—st.2 & 4	**11:23-28**	# 5		# 360

2 CORINTHIANS

Ref	Hymn	Ref	Hymn	Ref	Hymn
1:9	# 103		# 78		# 291—st.4
1:10	# 215—st.4		# 169	**5:7**	# 80
1:12	# 146		# 170—st.1		# 162
1:20	# 114		# 214—st.2		# 167
	# 193—st.5		# 253		# 222
	# 344—st.1	**4:4**	# 19		# 238
	# 345		# 59		# 346
1:20-22	# 301		# 304		# 369
1:22	# 64—st.3	**4:4-6**	# 56	**5:8**	# 78
1:24	# 80		# 357		# 98—st.3
	# 167	**4:6**	# 43—st.3		# 152—st.5
	# 238		# 67—st.2		# 153
	# 346		# 78		# 169
2:4	# 124		# 101		# 183—st.1
	# 230		# 102		# 253
2:11	# 4—st.3		# 119—st.2		# 259
	# 167—st.2		# 124		# 313
2:14	# 80		# 152—st.5		# 324—st.3
	# 154		# 159		# 368
	# 190		# 183—st.1	**5:9**	# 127
	# 197		# 195		# 311
	# 207—st.3		# 204		# 378—st.3
	# 211		# 210	**5:9-10**	# 1—st.3
	# 264—st.2		# 248—st.2		# 88
	# 295		# 279		# 245
	# 300		# 296	**5:10**	# 326
	# 345		# 315—st.2	**5:13-14**	# 214
	# 375		# 342		# 251—st.3
3:2	# 76		# 345		# 337
3:3	# 298		# 346	**5:14**	# 186
3:4-5	# 344		# 347		# 364
	# 346		# 358—st.3	**5:14-15**	# 180
3:5	# 1—st.4	**4:10**	# 37	**5:15**	# 9
	# 15	**4:10-11**	# 174		# 24
	# 71		# 205		# 142
	# 180—st.1		# 215—st.4		# 156
	# 218		# 340—st.3		# 218
3:6	# 48	**4:14**	# 144		# 312—st.3
	# 62	**4:16**	# 4—st.2	**5:17**	# 41
	# 112		# 26		# 108
	# 298		# 178		# 124—st.2
3:17	# 133—st.4		# 279		# 214—st.4
	# 188	**4:18**	# 129		# 374—st.4
	# 214—st.3	**5:1**	# 36		# 379
3:18	# 48		# 228—st.5	**5:18**	# 163

GALATIANS

1:10	# 97—st.2		# 163	**4:8**	# 237
1:15	# 19		# 217	**4:23**	# 301
	# 111		# 262—st.2	**4:28**	# 301
1:23	# 81		# 275	**5:1**	# 154
2:4	# 286—st.3		# 289—st.2		# 214—st.2
2:10	# 370		# 291		# 240—st.4
2:16	# 167		# 328		# 244—st.2
	# 263		# 345		# 266
	# 344		# 364		# 349—st.3
2:19-20	# 218	**3:14**	# 346—st.2	**5:2**	# 87—st.3
2:20	# 22	**3:14-22**	# 301	**5:5**	# 48
	# 28	**3:16**	# 373—st.3		# 329
	# 36	**3:22**	# 178—st.3	**5:6**	# 238
	# 80		# 238	**5:7**	# 34
	# 122	**3:26**	# 37		# 56—st.3
	# 140		# 51	**5:11**	# 164
	# 142		# 52		# 328
	# 152	**3:26-28**	# 161		# 366
	# 154		# 264—st.3	**5:13**	# 1
	# 157		# 314		# 87—st.3
	# 163	**3:27**	# 218		# 88
	# 167	**3:28**	# 44		# 97
	# 174		# 56		# 121
	# 178		# 157		# 161
	# 186		# 199		# 214—st.2
	# 196		# 232		# 216
	# 205	**3:29**	# 2		# 232
	# 215—st.4		# 301		# 245
	# 242	**4:1-7**	# 2		# 249
	# 262	**4:4**	# 65		# 287
	# 275		# 94		# 355—st.4
	# 280		# 189	**5:16**	# 237
	# 289—st.2		# 303		# 347
	# 323		# 341	**5:17**	# 178—st.3
	# 344	**4:4-5**	# 123	**5:17-18**	# 48
	# 355—st.2		# 146		# 133
3:2	# 62		# 163		# 298
	# 133		# 291	**5:18**	# 310—st.4
	# 146—st.3	**4:4-7**	# 37—st.2 & 4	**5:22**	# 62
3:4	# 170—st.1		# 63—st.3		# 63—st.3
3:5	# 63—st.3		# 120—st.3	**5:22-23**	# 3—st.4
3:13	# 6		# 275		# 48
	# 31—st.3	**4:6**	# 24—st.5		# 112
	# 116		# 135—st.2		# 133
	# 123	**4:7**	# 41	**5:24**	# 140

EPHESIANS

2:4-8	# 275	**2:14**	# 70—st.3		# 298—st.1
2:4-9	# 19		# 344—st.3	**3:16-17**	# 153
	# 111	**2:14-17**	# 268	**3:16-19**	# 178
	# 263	**2:14-18**	# 284	**3:17**	# 126—refrain
2:5-6	# 167	**2:16**	# 135—last st.		# 184
2:7-8	# 146		# 140		# 218
2:8	# 135—st.2		# 320—st.3 & 4	**3:17-19**	# 152
	# 139—st.3		# 328		# 160
	# 178—st.4	**2:18**	# 43—st.2		# 183
	# 282		# 63—st.3		# 186
	# 344		# 246		# 248
2:10	# 1		# 340—st.1		# 287
	# 88		# 345		# 364
	# 97	**2:19**	# 37—st.2	**3:17-20**	# 15
	# 108	**2:19-20**	# 131—st.3	**3:18-19**	# 214
	# 205	**2:19-22**	# 50		# 320—st.2
	# 216		# 188	**3:19**	# 157
	# 249		# 254		# 187
	# 281		# 314		# 219
2:12	# 135	**2:20**	# 28—st.2		# 303
2:12-13	# 301		# 137	**3:20-21**	# 345
2:13	# 6	**2:20-22**	# 55	**3:21**	# 87—st.4
	# 7		# 148		# 254
	# 24	**3:6**	# 2		# 316
	# 30—st.4		# 41	**4:1**	# 1
	# 42—st.3		# 54		# 237
	# 75—st.4		# 301		# 347
	# 116—st.2	**3:6-8**	# 91	**4:1-7**	# 37
	# 164	**3:8**	# 54	**4:2-3**	# 44
	# 177		# 135	**4:3**	# 48
	# 193		# 193		# 125
	# 217—st.2	**3:10**	# 104	**4:3-6**	# 56
	# 229	**3:10-12**	# 101		# 161
	# 240—st.4		# 256—st.4		# 264—st.3
	# 244—st.2	**3:11**	# 258	**4:4-6**	# 314—st.2
	# 269—st.2	**3:12**	# 41	**4:6**	# 73
	# 282		# 222		# 107
	# 329		# 329		# 230—st.3
	# 333		# 340—st.1		# 256
	# 335	**3:14**	# 100	**4:7**	# 19
	# 361—st.2	**3:14-15**	# 207		# 111
	# 366	**3:16**	# 61		# 137
2:13-18	# 29		# 76—st.2	**4:8-10**	# 262
	# 334		# 122—st.4		# 320
2:13-22	# 37		# 133—st.3	**4:10**	# 70

	# 119		# 162—st.3		# 154
	# 217—st.3		# 192—st.2		# 155
4:11-12	# 93		# 237		# 182—st.4
4:13	# 79—st.1		# 347		# 201
	# 90—st.3		# 369		# 240
	# 198—st.4	**5:8-9**	# 134		# 277
4:13-15	# 219	**5:8-14**	# 37—st.1		# 356
4:14	# 193—st.3		# 101	**5:20**	# 309
4:15	# 55		# 323		# 345
	# 76—st.2	**5:9**	# 112	**5:21-33**	# 118
	# 265—st.3		# 133		# 243
4:15-16	# 314	**5:14**	# 56		# 250
4:17	# 303—last st.		# 67—st.2	**5:23**	# 314
4:18	# 19		# 128	**5:23-24**	# 55
4:20-21	# 212		# 143—st.3	**5:23-32**	# 148
4:21	# 340—st.2		# 176		# 188
4:23	# 26		# 215—st.4		# 314
	# 239		# 248—st.2	**5:25**	# 87—st.3 & 4
	# 279		# 305		# 152
4:24	# 108		# 327	**5:25-27**	# 314
	# 310		# 357	**5:26**	# 191
4:25	# 264—st.3	**5:14-15**	# 347		# 321
	# 265—st.3	**5:15**	# 198		# 374
4:27	# 130—st.3		# 237	**6:1-4**	# 118
4:28	# 370		# 261		# 243
4:30	# 74—st.2		# 369		# 250
4:32	# 319—st.2	**5:17**	# 1—st.2	**6:2**	# 301
5:1-2	# 37		# 76	**6:6**	# 76
	# 249		# 88		# 141—st.2
	# 311		# 97—st.1		# 223
5:2	# 24		# 122		# 286—st.4
	# 29		# 141—st.2		# 308
	# 108—st.4		# 219		# 370
	# 152		# 223	**6:7**	# 1
	# 182—st.3		# 265		# 88
	# 186		# 372		# 97
	# 220	**5:18**	# 48		# 121
	# 262		# 61		# 216
	# 288		# 62		# 281
	# 334—refrain		# 133		# 355—st.4
5:4	# 68		# 298	**6:10**	# 1—st.4
	# 230	**5:19**	# 28		# 102
	# 352		# 60		# 175
5:6	# 261		# 79—st.2		# 192—st.3
5:8	# 128		# 124		# 361—st.4

	# 278		# 307		# 265
	# 342		# 360	**1:10**	# 1
	# 351	**4:7**	# 124—st.1		# 205
	# 357		# 211		# 216
	# 378		# 226		# 245
2:16	# 47		# 268		# 249
	# 194		# 284		# 281
	# 255—st.4	**4:8**	# 87		# 369
	# 377		# 108	**1:11**	# 187—st.2
3:1	# 126—st.3		# 192—st.4		# 192—st.3
3:3	# 220	**4:13**	# 71		# 222—st.2
3:3-11	# 164		# 104		# 324—st.2
	# 366		# 175		# 361—st.4
3:7-11	# 98		# 187—st.2	**1:11-14**	# 7
3:8	# 219		# 324		# 30
	# 320—st.2		# 361—st.4		# 67—st.2
3:9	# 329	**4:19**	# 93		# 75
	# 344		# 109		# 155
3:10	# 126		# 115		# 324
	# 196—st.4		# 150	**1:12**	# 68
	# 221		# 158		# 69
3:12	# 37		# 184		# 187—st.2
3:12-14	# 34		# 193—st.4	**1:12-13**	# 28—st.3
3:13	# 113—st.3		# 322—st.1	**1:12-14**	# 163
3:13-14	# 130		# 352		# 240—st.4
3:14	# 1—st.4	**4:20**	# 345		# 275
	# 84	**4:23**	# 208		# 291
	# 368			**1:13**	# 4—st.3
3:18	# 164	**COLOSSIANS**			# 162—st.3
	# 177	**1:5**	# 47—st.2 & 3		# 184
	# 197		# 78	**1:13-14**	# 244
	# 300		# 213—st.1		# 334—st.3
	# 366		# 228—st.5	**1:13-17**	# 159
3:20-21	# 145		# 241	**1:13-23**	# 368
	# 168		# 253	**1:14**	# 23
	# 206		# 255—st.4		# 42—st.3
	# 363—st.1		# 291—st.4		# 154
4:3	# 320—st.3		# 321—st.4		# 178—st.4
4:4	# 60		# 329		# 193
	# 242		# 368		# 217
	# 248—st.3	**1:8**	# 62		# 229
	# 276		# 63—st.3		# 242
	# 277		# 87—st.3		# 333
4:5	# 363—st.3	**1:9**	# 141—st.2		# 335
4:6	# 274		# 219	**1:15-19**	# 11

COLOSSIANS

Verse	Ref	Verse	Ref	Verse	Ref
1:15-20	# 182		# 314		# 165—st.2
	# 215	**1:27**	# 104	**3:3-4**	# 218
	# 273		# 135	**3:4**	# 124—st.5
	# 276		# 183		# 138—st.4
1:16	# 258		# 329		# 146—st.4
1:16-17	# 210	**1:28**	# 81		# 253
1:17	# 31—st.2		# 198—st.4		# 302—st.4
1:18	# 50	**1:29**	# 324—st.2		# 304—st.4
	# 55	**2:2**	# 41		# 363
	# 188		# 44	**3:10**	# 239
	# 254		# 87—st.3	**3:11**	# 44
	# 314		# 190		# 56
1:20	# 116—st.2	**2:3**	# 380—st.4		# 91
	# 140	**2:4**	# 359		# 135
	# 217—st.2	**2:5**	# 18		# 161
	# 229		# 225		# 214—st.2
	# 244—st.2	**2:6**	# 127		# 232
	# 320—st.3 & 4		# 198—st.4		# 264—st.3
	# 335		# 347	**3:13**	# 310—st.2
	# 361—st.2	**2:6-7**	# 369	**3:14**	# 87—st.4
	# 374	**2:7**	# 50	**3:15**	# 68
1:20-21	# 163		# 68		# 69
	# 242		# 69		# 198—st.1
	# 275		# 222		# 230
	# 291		# 230		# 264—st.3
1:20-22	# 6		# 238		# 268
	# 185		# 352		# 284
1:20-23	# 7	**2:9-10**	# 214—st.1	**3:15-17**	# 52
	# 29	**2:13**	# 147	**3:16**	# 28—st.2
	# 30		# 319—st.2		# 60
	# 75	**2:13-15**	# 167—st.3		# 79—st.2
	# 164		# 328		# 124
	# 177	**2:14**	# 163		# 154
	# 251		# 242		# 155
	# 268		# 275		# 182—st.4
	# 282	**2:15**	# 3—st.3		# 201
	# 328		# 135—last st.		# 240
	# 333		# 338—st.3		# 277
	# 334		# 363—st.2		# 356
1:21	# 322—st.3	**3:1**	# 70	**3:17**	# 88
1:23	# 91		# 276		# 179
	# 135	**3:1-15**	# 214		# 230
	# 225	**3:2**	# 4		# 309
	# 238		# 82		# 345
1:24	# 188		# 153	**3:18-21**	# 118

1 THESSALONIANS

	# 352
5:21	# 160—last st.
	# 192—st. 3 & 4
	# 344—refrain
5:21-22	# 261
5:22	# 104—st.2
5:23	# 22—st.3
	# 51—st.4
	# 153
	# 284—st.4
	# 308
5:24	# 107
	# 114
	# 176
	# 193
	# 266
5:28	# 208

2 THESSALONIANS

1:3	# 238
1:7	# 253
	# 283—st.1
1:7-10	# 168
	# 206—st.3
	# 326
1:12	# 19
	# 42
	# 139
	# 244
	# 308
	# 380—st.1
2	# 363
2:13	# 9—st.4
	# 11—st.2
2:14	# 266
2:16	# 74
	# 135
	# 180
	# 329
	# 368
2:16-17	# 66
	# 71
	# 226
	# 324

2:17	# 18—st.4
3:3	# 36
	# 51
	# 102
	# 241
	# 286—st.2
	# 306
3:4	# 222
3:5	# 162
	# 310
3:16	# 70—st.3
	# 208
	# 268
	# 284
3:18	# 208

1 TIMOTHY

1:1	# 135
	# 329
1:2	# 208
	# 268
	# 284
1:8	# 316—last st.
1:12	# 88
	# 175
	# 245
	# 251—st.3
	# 311
	# 324
1:14	# 19
	# 64
	# 111
1:14-15	# 57
	# 74
	# 180
1:14-17	# 159
	# 270
	# 345
1:15	# 7
	# 123
	# 163
	# 242
	# 266
	# 275

	# 291
1:15-19	# 277
1:16	# 212
	# 288
	# 310—st.2
1:17	# 82
	# 151
	# 201
	# 276
	# 292
	# 318
1:17-19	# 197
1:18	# 127
1:18-19	# 18
	# 84
	# 225
	# 264
	# 295
	# 300
2:1	# 360
2:1-2	# 105
	# 208
	# 284
2:5	# 24
	# 43—st.2
	# 147
	# 329
	# 340—st.1
2:5-6	# 116—st.2
	# 185
	# 334
	# 361
2:6	# 163
	# 242
	# 275
	# 291
	# 312—st.3
	# 345
2:8	# 274
	# 307
	# 360
3:15	# 148
	# 188
	# 254
	# 314

3:16	# 63—st.2		# 380		# 146
	# 262	**6:19**	# 86		# 167—st.2
	# 279	**6:21**	# 208		# 184
4:6	# 45				# 344
	# 255—st.4	**2 TIMOTHY**		**1:12-13**	# 346
4:6-12	# 310			**1:13**	# 212
4:8	# 301	**1:1**	# 301	**1:13-14**	# 37
4:10	# 102	**1:2**	# 268		# 63—st.3
	# 211	**1:7**	# 63—st.3		# 214
	# 344		# 104	**1:14**	# 112
4:12	# 192		# 108		# 133
4:14	# 93		# 133		# 297
	# 272		# 153	**2:1**	# 15—st.2
5:8	# 118		# 186		# 19
	# 243		# 287		# 96—st.2
6:4-5	# 56—st.3		# 298		# 124—st.3
6:6	# 73		# 303—last st.		# 137
6:12	# 18	**1:8**	# 149		# 278—st.3
	# 80		# 221		# 329—st.2
	# 84		# 357	**2:1-4**	# 375
	# 86		# 378	**2:2**	# 212
	# 104	**1:9**	# 19	**2:3-4**	# 18
	# 127		# 57		# 80
	# 197		# 73		# 84
	# 225		# 111		# 104
	# 277		# 293		# 197
	# 264	**1:9-10**	# 266		# 225
	# 300		# 269—st.2		# 264
	# 320—st.3	**1:10**	# 27—st.3		# 295
	# 330		# 42—st.3		# 300
	# 375		# 53		# 330
6:15	# 139—st.4		# 70—st.2	**2:4**	# 127
	# 207		# 99—st.4	**2:7**	# 303—last st.
	# 375		# 115—st.3	**2:8**	# 126
6:15-16	# 39		# 126		# 144
	# 63		# 144		# 262
	# 70		# 242		# 320
	# 116—st.4		# 262		# 339
	# 159		# 332—st.2		# 373—st.3
	# 256		# 340—st.3	**2:9**	# 51—st.4
	# 270	**1:12**	# 41		# 145—st.2
	# 363—refrain		# 51—st.4	**2:10**	# 225
6:16	# 79		# 55—st.3		# 253
	# 269		# 80	**2:11**	# 218
	# 303		# 123	**2:12**	# 55—st.3

	# 124—st.5		# 206		# 30
	# 165		# 326		# 75
	# 171		# 363—st.1		# 142
	# 320	**4:17-18**	# 295		# 154
	# 363		# 361—st.4		# 163
2:13	# 107	**4:18**	# 51—st.4		# 164
	# 114		# 55—st.3		# 205
2:19	# 55		# 266		# 275
	# 114	**4:22**	# 183		# 291
	# 137		# 184—st.4		# 328
	# 179				# 333
	# 309				# 334
	# 314	**TITUS**			# 361
2:20-21	# 308	**1:2**	# 169	**3:3-7**	# 29
2:21	# 34		# 170		# 33
	# 216		# 259		# 63
2:22	# 73		# 301		# 214
2:24-25	# 212—st.2		# 368		# 337
2:26	# 266	**1:4**	# 268	**3:5**	# 108—st.1
3:15	# 47—st.3	**1:15**	# 108		# 269—st.2
	# 146—st.2	**2:4**	# 87—st.3		# 286—st.3
3:15-16	# 45		# 242		# 380—st.2
	# 194	**2:4-5**	# 118	**3:5-6**	# 61
	# 213		# 243		# 180
3:15-17	# 83		# 250		# 185
3:16	# 47	**2:7**	# 34—st.2		# 193
3:16-17	# 321	**2:8**	# 212		# 229
3:17	# 198—st.4	**2:11**	# 19		# 275
4:1	# 206		# 57		# 279
	# 326		# 74		# 297
4:5	# 97		# 111		# 335
4:7	# 80		# 178—st.4		# 374
	# 81		# 278—st.3	**3:5-7**	# 23
	# 86	**2:13**	# 41		# 24
	# 104		# 126—st.2		# 41
4:7-8	# 18		# 145		# 57
	# 84		# 168		# 111
	# 197		# 183—st.1		# 134—st.2
	# 225		# 206		# 163
	# 264		# 215—st.1		# 361
	# 295		# 262—st.5	**3:7**	# 2
	# 300		# 269—st.3		# 19
	# 330		# 329		# 70—st.2
4:8	# 124—st.5		# 363—refrain		# 86
	# 197—st.3	**2:14**	# 7		# 135

HEBREWS

4:7	# 341	**6:5**	# 83	**7:26-28**	# 139—st.4
4:9	# 4		# 255		# 289—st.3
	# 14		# 377	**7:27**	# 144—st.2
	# 15—st.3	**6:9-10**	# 88		# 333
	# 57		# 107		# 334
	# 86		# 108—st.4		# 345
	# 141—st.4		# 208—st.2		# 361
	# 198—st.4		# 281	**7:27-28**	# 116—st.2
	# 209	**6:10**	# 1	**8:1**	# 139—st.4
	# 253		# 245		# 269—st.3
	# 263	**6:11**	# 41		# 289
4:11	# 378—st.3		# 296	**8:6**	# 329—st.3
4:12	# 191—last st.	**6:11-12**	# 238		# 340
	# 194	**6:12-17**	# 301	**8:6-12**	# 301
	# 213	**6:13-19**	# 3	**8:12**	# 147
4:14	# 144—st.3	**6:17-19**	# 329		# 293
	# 276—st.2	**6:18-19**	# 26	**8:13**	# 329—st.3
4:14-16	# 139—st.3&4		# 135	**9:6-28**	# 244—st.2
4:15	# 150		# 241		# 361
	# 324—st.2	**6:19**	# 41	**9:11-26**	# 75
4:15-16	# 244—st.4	**6:20**	# 139—st.4		# 282
4:16	# 24		# 289—st.3		# 328
	# 66	**7:2**	# 350		# 333
	# 71	**7:9**	# 350		# 366
	# 90	**7:17**	# 139—st.4	**9:11-28**	# 6
	# 95	**7:19**	# 76		# 7
	# 104		# 141		# 30
	# 150		# 227	**9:12**	# 242
	# 178—st.4	**7:24**	# 36—st.2		# 275
	# 226		# 258	**9:12-14**	# 335
	# 278—st.3	**7:25**	# 24	**9:12-22**	# 116—st.2
	# 286—st.3		# 42—st.3		# 217—st.2
5:5-6	# 139—st.4		# 123		# 240—st.4
	# 289—st.3		# 144		# 269—st.2
5:7	# 152—st.2 & 3		# 242		# 361
5:8	# 6		# 244—st.2	**9:12-28**	# 42—st.3
	# 31—st.3		# 263	**9:13-14**	# 41
	# 142—st.3		# 266	**9:14**	# 23
	# 251		# 269		# 57—st.3
5:8-9	# 116		# 275		# 63—st.3
5:9	# 380—st.2		# 278		# 111—st.2
5:10	# 139—st.4		# 288		# 140
	# 289—st.3		# 291		# 167—st.2
5:12	# 212	**7:26**	# 37		# 180
6:3	# 76		# 276—st.2		# 185

	# 222		# 324—st.3		# 309
	# 251	**13:6**	# 104		# 352
	# 262		# 158		# 356
	# 328		# 165		# 380
12:2-3	# 196		# 199	**13:15-16**	# 308
12:2-4	# 6		# 241	**13:16**	# 350—st.4
	# 320	**13:8**	# 79	**13:20**	# 139—st.4
12:5-7	# 349—st.1		# 113		# 335
12:10	# 239		# 144—st.4	**13:20-21**	# 125
12:13	# 198		# 184—st.2		# 198
12:14	# 82		# 258		# 208
	# 310		# 269		# 269
12:22	# 96		# 318		# 284
	# 147—st.4	**13:9**	# 64		# 286—st.4
	# 169	**13:10**	# 164		# 325
	# 170		# 366		# 333
	# 267	**13:10-12**	# 333		# 361
	# 313	**13:10-14**	# 334	**13:21**	# 76
	# 356	**13:12**	# 42—st.3		# 82
12:23	# 191		# 116—st.2		# 122
12:24	# 24—st.2		# 217—st.2		# 141—st.2
	# 42		# 229		# 192
	# 116—st.2		# 240—st.4		# 212
	# 185		# 269—st.2		# 223
	# 217		# 335		# 308
	# 229		# 361		
	# 240—st.4	**13:12-15**	# 41	**JAMES**	
	# 269—st.2	**13:14**	# 302—st.4	**1:2**	# 165
	# 329—st.3		# 304—st.4	**1:4**	# 198—st.4
	# 333		# 319—st.2	**1:5**	# 93
	# 335		# 324—st.3		# 104
	# 340	**13:15**	# 28	**1:6**	# 15
	# 361		# 42		# 181
12:26	# 301		# 43—st.2		# 238
12:28	# 141—st.2		# 60		# 346
	# 299—st.2		# 68	**1:12**	# 130—st.3
12:29	# 210		# 69		# 225
13:1	# 44		# 75		# 300
	# 87—st.3		# 87—st.4		# 301
	# 232		# 89	**1:17**	# 51—st.3 & 4
13:4	# 250		# 149		# 87
13:5	# 99		# 201		# 101
	# 124		# 230		# 114
	# 292—st.3		# 272		# 124—st.4
13:5-6	# 137		# 292		# 159

	# 190—st.1	**4:15**	# 1—st.2		# 135
	# 203		# 76		# 154
	# 210		# 88		# 173
	# 296		# 97		# 252
	# 352		# 122		# 329
1:21	# 47—st.3		# 223	**1:3-4**	# 279
1:22-25	# 194		# 286—st.4	**1:3-5**	# 86
1:27	# 73		# 372—st.2		# 144
	# 214—st.4	**5:7-9**	# 168		# 170
	# 232		# 326		# 253
2:5	# 2		# 363		# 259
	# 301	**5:8**	# 126—st.2		# 368
2:8	# 87—st.3		# 144—st.4	**1:3-6**	# 39
2:14-16	# 369		# 204		# 108
2:22	# 198—st.4	**5:9**	# 82		# 145
2:24	# 177		# 246		# 337
2:26	# 308	**5:11**	# 18—st.4	**1:4**	# 2
3:2	# 198—st.4		# 225	**1:4-5**	# 222—st.4
3:7-12	# 39	**5:13**	# 28—st.2	**1:5**	# 51—st.4
3:16	# 82		# 41—refrain		# 55—st.3
3:17	# 112—st.2		# 42		# 218
4:1	# 82		# 52		# 286—st.2
4:4	# 165—st.2		# 60		# 306
4:4-5	# 82		# 201	**1:6**	# 363—refrain
4:4-6	# 214		# 240	**1:6-9**	# 28
	# 324		# 291	**1:7**	# 238
4:6	# 56—st.3		# 356	**1:7-9**	# 41
	# 335—st.2	**5:13-16**	# 274		# 333
4:7	# 140—st.3		# 307	**1:8**	# 149—st.1
	# 153		# 360		# 220
	# 167—st.2	**5:15**	# 122—st.3		# 242
	# 174	**5:16**	# 44		# 303—st.1
	# 278—st.3	**5:17**	# 135		# 320—st.2
	# 308			**1:8-9**	# 184—st.3
	# 375	**1 PETER**		**1:10**	# 19
4:8	# 76			**1:11**	# 217
	# 141	**1:2**	# 48	**1:13**	# 135
	# 209		# 63—st.3		# 145
	# 226		# 131—st.4		# 363
	# 227		# 229	**1:14**	# 106
	# 239		# 333	**1:15-16**	# 132
4:10	# 155—st.4		# 335		# 310
	# 184—st.4		# 361	**1:17**	# 107
	# 239	**1:2-6**	# 345		# 159
4:13-15	# 296—st.2	**1:3**	# 126		# 345

1 PETER

1:18-19	# 24—st.2	**2:6**	# 137		# 116—st.2
	# 42—st.3	**2:7**	# 139—st.3		# 152
	# 116—st.2		# 184		# 154
	# 154—st.2	**2:9**	# 11—st.2		# 155—st.3
	# 185		# 54		# 156
	# 217—st.2		# 60		# 164
	# 229		# 73		# 205
	# 240—st.4		# 89		# 217
	# 242		# 101		# 240—st.4
	# 244—st.2		# 131		# 242
	# 269—st.2		# 193		# 244—st.2
	# 275		# 195		# 251
	# 319—st.3		# 212		# 275
	# 333		# 266		# 282
	# 361		# 292		# 328—st.3
1:19	# 193		# 299—st.1		# 332—st.4
	# 222		# 304		# 334
1:21	# 164		# 323		# 361
	# 183—st.3		# 347		# 366
	# 241	**2:11**	# 127	**2:24-25**	# 163
	# 366		# 261		# 289
1:22	# 73	**2:12**	# 216	**2:25**	# 38—st.2
	# 87—st.3	**2:15**	# 223		# 64—st.3
	# 232	**2:17**	# 44		# 139—st.4
1:22-23	# 7—st.4		# 161		# 178
	# 30—st.4		# 190—st.3		# 269—st.1
	# 75—st.4		# 281		# 286—st.2
	# 108		# 299—st.2		# 306
	# 214—st.4	**2:21**	# 37		# 322—st.3
1:23	# 379		# 97	**3:1**	# 118
1:24-25	# 255		# 98		# 243
	# 321		# 147—st.2	**3:7**	# 118
1:25	# 29—st.2		# 156		# 243
2:1	# 82		# 175—st.3		# 250
2:2	# 47—st.3		# 205	**3:8**	# 44
	# 194		# 245		# 190—st.3
	# 219		# 249		# 232
	# 255		# 288		# 370
	# 310—st.1		# 310—st.2	**3:8-12**	# 261
	# 377		# 311—st.3	**3:12**	# 43
2:3	# 41		# 372		# 55—st.2
2:4	# 269—st.2	**2:21-24**	# 142		# 274
2:4-7	# 50		# 174		# 307
	# 314	**2:22-25**	# 180		# 360
2:5	# 288	**2:24**	# 28—st.2 & 4	**3:15**	# 28

Ref.	Hymn	Ref.	Hymn	Ref.	Hymn
	# 135		# 269—st.3		# 139
	# 149		# 367		# 155—st.4
	# 239	**4:12**	# 124—st.4		# 158
	# 257		# 137		# 165
	# 329	**4:12-13**	# 98		# 218
	# 357		# 251		# 240
	# 378		# 328—st.4		# 244—st.4
3:17-18	# 174	**4:13**	# 6		# 296—st.3
3:18	# 6		# 78—st.2 & 3		# 307
	# 62		# 152—st.5		# 325
	# 63		# 168—st.4		# 360
	# 116		# 196—st.4	**5:7-9**	# 84
	# 132		# 217		# 167
	# 142		# 248—st.3 & 4	**5:8**	# 104—st.2
	# 152—st.4		# 253	**5:8-9**	# 18
	# 242		# 269—st.3		# 130—st.3
	# 251		# 363		# 197
	# 269—st.2		# 368—st.3		# 264—st.2
	# 275	**4:16**	# 171		# 295
	# 282	**4:19**	# 82		# 300
	# 328		# 99—st.3		# 330
	# 334		# 124—st.4		# 375
	# 345		# 218	**5:9**	# 346
	# 361		# 288	**5:10**	# 51
3:20	# 278—st.2		# 324		# 73
3:22	# 70—st.1	**5:1**	# 253		# 198—st.4
	# 119		# 263—st.4		# 311—st.2
	# 207	**5:3**	# 34—st.2		# 320—st.3
	# 217—st.4	**5:4**	# 124—st.5	**5:10-11**	# 284
	# 262—st.4		# 197—st.3		# 345
	# 269		# 225—st.3	**5:11**	# 269
	# 276—st.2		# 253		# 292
	# 341—st.5		# 269—st.1	**5:14**	# 208
	# 380—st.3		# 300—st.4		# 284
4:3	# 237		# 306		
4:7	# 274		# 325	**2 PETER**	
	# 363		# 363		
4:8	# 232	**5:5**	# 239	**1:2**	# 64
4:10	# 57	**5:6**	# 113		# 208
	# 64	**5:7**	# 71	**1:3**	# 184
	# 288		# 90		# 266
4:10-11	# 1		# 95	**1:4**	# 3
	# 54		# 99		# 301
	# 93		# 109		# 310
4:11	# 265		# 125	**1:5**	# 219

2 PETER

	# 303—last st.
1:5-8	# 108
1:7	# 87—st.3
1:9	# 19
	# 23
1:10	# 11—st.2
1:16	# 145
	# 363—st.1
1:17	# 326
1:19	# 4—last st.
	# 32
	# 56—st.1
	# 83
	# 194
	# 210
	# 255
	# 321
	# 342
	# 367
1:19-21	# 45
	# 213
1:20-21	# 47—st.4
1:21	# 112
	# 321
2:9	# 165
	# 214—st.3
	# 349
3:3-14	# 168
	# 206
	# 326
	# 363
3:4	# 301
3:8	# 241—st.4
3:9	# 97
	# 257—st.1
	# 278—st.2
	# 301
3:10	# 146—st.4
3:12	# 348
	# 301
	# 304—st.4
	# 338—st.3
3:13-14	# 214—st.4
3:14	# 363—st.3
3:15	# 278—st.2

3:17	# 130
	# 225
3:18	# 64
	# 124—st.3
	# 219
	# 269
	# 345

1 JOHN

1:1-2	# 340—st.3
1:2	# 70
	# 215—st.4
1:3	# 141
	# 175
	# 184
	# 132
1:4	# 377
1:5	# 43—st.3
	# 102
	# 210
	# 248—st.2
	# 257—st.1
	# 305
	# 342
1:5-7	# 101
	# 159
	# 190
	# 195
	# 323
	# 347
1:5-9	# 237
1:6	# 227—st.2
1:7	# 42—st.3
	# 44
	# 128
	# 240—st.4
	# 244—st.2
	# 275
	# 337
	# 344—st.2
	# 380—st.2
1:7-9	# 7
	# 23
	# 30

	# 57
	# 75
	# 111
	# 114—st.3
	# 193
	# 229
	# 319—st.3
	# 324—st.1
	# 335
	# 374
1:8-9	# 242
1:8-10	# 178—st.3
1:9	# 73
	# 140
	# 180
	# 263
	# 286—st.3
	# 361—st.2 & 3
2:1	# 144—st.2
	# 340—st.1
2:1-2	# 24
	# 222
	# 329
2:2	# 42—st.3
	# 147
	# 152
	# 154
2:5-6	# 153
	# 198
2:6	# 97—st.1
	# 124—st.4
	# 245
	# 262—st.1
	# 311
	# 369
2:8	# 56
	# 128
	# 143—st.3
	# 248—st.2
	# 305
	# 323
	# 347
	# 357
2:9	# 184—st.4
2:10	# 232

2:11	# 19—st.1		214		# 350
2:12	# 179	**3:2**	# 41		# 370
	# 309		# 51	**3:22**	# 286—st.4
	# 319—st.2		# 52	**3:23**	# 263
2:13	# 105		# 58—st.4	**3:24**	# 4
	# 277		# 78		# 48
2:14	# 264—st.2		# 145—st.2		# 61
	# 375		# 169		# 133
2:15-16	# 165—st.2		# 253		# 297
2:17	# 1		# 259		# 298
	# 82		# 324—st.3		# 304—st.3
	# 88		# 368	**4:1**	# 344—refrain
	# 175—st.4	**3:3**	# 79—st.2 & 3	**4:4**	# 37—st.2
	# 212—st.4		# 108		# 295—st.3
	# 223		# 329	**4:6**	# 112
	# 369	**3:5**	# 262	**4:7**	# 108
	# 372—st.2		# 334—st.4		# 133—st.2
2:20	# 133	**3:6**	# 226—st.1		# 379
2:23	# 79—st.1	**3:8**	# 101	**4:7-8**	# 87—st.3
2:25	# 144—st.2		# 167—st.2	**4:7-18**	# 162
	# 145		# 338—st.3	**4:7-21**	# 101
	# 169		# 363—st.2		# 108
	# 170	**3:9**	# 379		# 214
	# 175—st.4	**3:10**	# 51		# 299—st.4
	# 253		# 52		# 337
	# 259	**3:11**	# 232	**4:9-10**	# 116—st.2
	# 301	**3:14**	# 124—st.2		# 149
	# 368	**3:16**	# 37		# 152
2:27	# 112		# 70—st.4		# 154
	# 219		# 97		# 155
2:28	# 41		# 108		# 244—st.2
	# 171		# 138—st.3		# 257—st.3
	# 363—st.3		# 142		# 269—st.2
2:29	# 379		# 156		# 275
3	# 37		# 157	**4:10**	# 29—st.4
3:1	# 24—st.4 & 5		# 160		# 146
	# 160		# 183—st.4		# 287
	# 162		# 186	**4:11**	# 87—st.3
	# 183—st.4		# 205		# 108
	# 186		# 232		# 232
	# 248—st.1		# 244—st.2	**4:12**	# 159
	# 275		# 287		# 198—st.4
	# 364		# 311—st.3	**4:13**	# 37
3:1-2	# 2		# 364		# 41
	# 101	**3:17**	# 16		# 48

1 JOHN

	# 63—st.3		# 379	**9**	# 37
	# 133	**5:2**	# 310—st.1		
	# 157	**5:4**	# 211	**3 JOHN**	
	# 187—st.5		# 238		
	# 226		# 264—st.2	**3**	# 81
	# 297		# 379		# 192
	# 298	**5:4-5**	# 15		# 198—st.2
	# 302		# 41		# 261
	# 310		# 54		# 265
4:14	# 123		# 80	**11**	# 108
	# 149		# 127		
	# 154		# 167	**JUDE**	
	# 217		# 295—st.3		
	# 291		# 300	**3**	# 18
	# 345		# 330		# 80
	# 361		# 346		# 81
4:15	# 79—st.1		# 375		# 84
	# 303	**5:6**	# 112		# 86
4:16	# 257—st.3		# 146—st.3		# 197
4:16-21	# 287		# 185		# 225
4:18	# 56—st.2	**5:7**	# 131—st.4		# 264
	# 139—st.1		# 139		# 300
	# 291—st.3		# 205		# 330
4:19	# 7	**5:11-12**	# 28—st.3		# 375
	# 30	**5:11-13**	# 70—st.2	**6**	# 3—st.3
	# 75	**5:12**	# 150—st.3		# 338—st.3
	# 119—st.2		# 156	**9**	# 167—st.2
	# 157		# 340—st.3	**14**	# 168—st.3
	# 160		# 355—st.2		# 206—st.1
	# 164	**5:13**	# 253		# 313
	# 186		# 368	**15**	# 326
	# 187	**5:14**	# 301	**20**	# 238
	# 222—st.2	**5:14-15**	# 274		# 297
	# 224		# 307	**21**	# 74
	# 244—refrain		# 360		# 162
	# 251	**5:15**	# 346—st.3	**24**	# 51—st.4
	# 286—st.4	**5:20**	# 37		# 55—st.3
	# 287		# 70—st.2		# 286—st.2
	# 364		# 344		# 306
4:21	# 44	**5:21**	# 237	**24-25**	# 108
	# 161				# 214—st.4
	# 232	**2 JOHN**			# 269
	# 370				# 273
5:1	# 263	**3**	# 284		# 353
	# 376	**4**	# 198—st.2		# 360

25	# 151
	# 155
	# 292

REVELATION

1:3	# 45
	# 42—st.3
	# 255
	# 280
	# 377
1:4	# 268
1:5	# 24
	# 42—st.3
	# 144
	# 154
	# 185
	# 240
	# 244—st.2
	# 344—st.2
	# 364
1:5-6	# 29
	# 41
	# 63
	# 70
	# 116
	# 269
	# 328
	# 333
	# 345
	# 361
	# 380
1:7	# 124—st.5
	# 204
	# 262—st.5
1:7-8	# 206
	# 363
1:8	# 70
	# 214—st.2
	# 258
	# 269—st.3
	# 318
1:9	# 184
1:10	# 236
1:11	# 318

1:16	# 59
	# 304
1:17	# 74—st.3
	# 369—last st.
1:17-18	# 70
1:18	# 115—st.3
	# 126
	# 144
	# 154—st.3
	# 215—st.4
	# 258
	# 276—st.3
	# 339—st.2
	# 358—st.1
2:7	# 188
	# 225
	# 295—st.3
	# 314—last st.
2:8	# 126
2:10	# 197—st.3
2:11	# 70—st.2
	# 295—st.3
2:17	# 99—st.2
	# 295—st.3
	# 324—st.3
2:26	# 295—st.3
2:28	# 49
	# 324—refrain
3:5	# 123—st.4
	# 170—st.3
	# 295—st.3
3:7-8	# 234
3:8	# 228—st.4
	# 246
	# 340—st.1
3:10	# 55—st.3
	# 150—st.2
3:11	# 18
3:12	# 169
	# 170
	# 320
3:19	# 349—st.1
3:20	# 143
	# 176
	# 193

	# 228—st.4
	# 246
	# 266
	# 293
	# 376
3:20-21	# 282
3:21	# 225
	# 300
4:1	# 246
4:2	# 38
	# 276—st.2
4:2-11	# 70
4:3	# 346—st.4
4:8	# 14
4:8-11	# 131
	# 132
	# 200
	# 236—st.4
4:9	# 230
4:11	# 8
	# 17
	# 151
	# 271
	# 273
	# 352—st.2
5:5	# 117
5:6	# 70
	# 116
5:9	# 54—st.4
	# 182—st.4
	# 275
	# 291
5:9-10	# 177
	# 282
	# 328
	# 333
	# 345
	# 361
	# 380
5:9-14	# 363
5:10	# 169
5:11	# 207—st.2&4
5:11-12	# 313
5:11-13	# 11
	# 60

REVELATION

	# 330—st.4		# 333		# 230
	# 378—st.3		# 335		# 270
5:11-14	# 132		# 344—st.2		# 280—st.4
	# 271		# 361		# 318
	# 367		# 374	**12:10**	# 182
5:12	# 42	**7:14-15**	# 180	**12:10-11**	# 338—st.3
	# 240	**7:14-17**	# 168—st.4	**12:11**	# 18
5:12-13	# 182	**7:15**	# 214—st.3 & 4		# 185
	# 215	**7:15-17**	# 26		# 225
	# 269		# 282		# 229
	# 279	**7:17**	# 15		# 295—st.3
	# 364		# 36—st.3		# 300
5:13	# 201		# 66—st.3		# 333
5:13-14	# 131		# 71		# 335
	# 318		# 78—st.3		# 375
6:9	# 330		# 95	**13:10**	# 249—st.3
6:11	# 86		# 96—st.2	**14:1-3**	# 356
6:14	# 167—st.4		# 125		# 364
7:9	# 86		# 143—st.2	**14:3**	# 182—st.4
7:9-10	# 182		# 178		# 380
	# 364		# 184	**14:3-5**	# 54—st.4
7:9-12	# 378—st.3		# 222	**14:6**	# 54
	# 380		# 259		# 56
7:9-17	# 54—st.4		# 289		# 91
	# 70		# 306		# 257
	# 115—st.3		# 322—st.2		# 278
	# 169	**9:9**	# 339—st.3 & 4		# 351
	# 170	**10:1**	# 168—st.3		# 357
	# 313		# 304		# 378
	# 319—st.3	**10:11**	# 357	**14:7**	# 8
	# 330—last st.	**11:15**	# 11		# 13
7:10	# 116		# 56—st.3		# 87
	# 240		# 70		# 107
7:11-12	# 11		# 119		# 292
	# 60		# 173		# 352—st.2
	# 207—st.2 & 4		# 182	**14:12**	# 249—st.3
	# 269—st.1		# 206—st.4	**14:12-13**	# 221— st.2 & 3
7:12	# 159		# 207	**14:13**	# 15—st.3
	# 230		# 264		# 25
7:14	# 23		# 276		# 57—st.2
	# 24—st.2		# 316—last st.		# 86
	# 111—st.2		# 378—st.3		# 88
	# 170	**11:15-17**	# 269—st.3		# 121—st.1
	# 185	**11:15-18**	# 326		# 141—st.4
	# 229	**11:17**	# 107		

	# 170	**19:1**	# 70	**21:2-5**	# 96
	# 198—st.4		# 353	**21:3**	# 214—st.1
	# 245	**19:1-7**	# 182	**21:4**	# 25
	# 253		# 269		# 36—st.3
	# 259		# 276		# 53
	# 368		# 332		# 78
14:14	# 206	**19:1-10**	# 380		# 93
14:15	# 68	**19:5**	# 60		# 99—st.4
	# 69	**19:6**	# 151		# 168—st.4
	# 121		# 313		# 169
15:2	# 170	**19:6-7**	# 63		# 220—st.3
15:2-4	# 13		# 256		# 222—st.2
	# 107		# 270		# 259
	# 114		# 273		# 363—st.2
	# 132		# 353	**21:6**	# 258
	# 159	**19:7-9**	# 148	**21:7**	# 127
	# 319—st.3		# 314—last st.		# 295—st.3
15:3	# 356	**19:9**	# 129	**21:9**	# 148
	# 364—last st.		# 169		# 314
15:3-4	# 380		# 170		# 363—st.1
15:4	# 89		# 306	**21:11**	# 346—st.4
	# 91	**19:12**	# 70	**21:18-19**	# 346—st.4
	# 131	**19:13**	# 31	**21:21**	# 368—st.4
	# 257		# 63—st.2	**21:22-25**	# 358—st.3
	# 316—last st.	**19:16**	# 11	**21:22-27**	# 59
16:5	# 107—st.3		# 182		# 101
	# 270		# 207—st.4		# 159
16:15	# 146—st.4		# 269—st.3		# 319
	# 168	**20**	# 326		# 323
	# 363—st.3	**20:4**	# 330	**21:23**	# 56
17:14	# 9—st.4	**20:6**	# 124—st.5		# 67
	# 11—st.2	**20:10**	# 3		# 79—st.3
	# 63		# 338—st.3		# 119
	# 70	**20:11**	# 38		# 143—st.3
	# 139—st.4		# 170		# 210
	# 197		# 276—st.2		# 305
	# 207	**20:12-15**	# 320—st.3		# 315—st.2
	# 256	**20:14**	# 276—st.3		# 357
	# 264		# 358—st.1	**21:23-24**	# 128
	# 295	**21**	# 169	**21:24**	# 237
	# 330		# 170	**21:25**	# 14
	# 339		# 313	**22**	# 170
	# 363	**21:1**	# 338—st.3		# 313
	# 375	**21:2**	# 170	**22:1**	# 96—st.2
18:8	# 191		# 356		# 177

REVELATION

	# 324		# 319		# 324
22:1-2	# 66		# 324—st.3	**22:17**	# 96—st.2
	# 115—st.2	**22:5**	# 55—st.3		# 143—st.2
22:3	# 70		# 210		# 176
	# 182		# 253		# 193
	# 315		# 259		# 246
22:3-4	# 207—st.3		# 323		# 266
22:3-5	# 119		# 368		# 293
	# 145—st.4	**22:10**	# 255—st.4		# 322—st.2
	# 206	**22:12**	# 168		# 376
22:4	# 22		# 326	**22:18-19**	# 45
	# 78	**22:13**	# 318		# 47—st.4
	# 139	**22:14**	# 38—st.3	**22:20**	# 168
	# 152—st.5	**22:16**	# 49		# 234
	# 179		# 79		# 262—st.5
	# 183—st.1		# 177—st.2		
	# 309		# 210	**22:21**	# 208

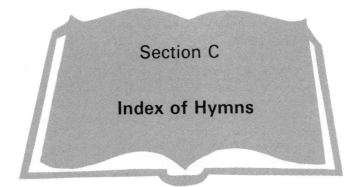

Section C

Index of Hymns